THE CLASSIC M1 GARAND

AN ONGOING LEGACY FOR SHOOTERS AND COLLECTORS

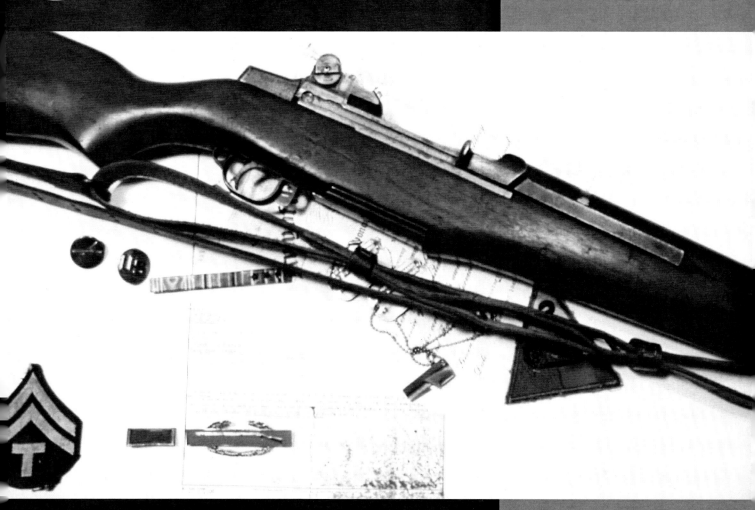

PALADIN PRESS · BOULDER, COLORADO

JIM THOMPSON

Also by Jim Thompson:

The Complete M1 Garand: A Guide for the Shooter and Collector

The Classic M1 Garand:
An Ongoing Legacy for Shooters and Collectors
by Jim Thompson

Copyright © 2001 by Jim Thompson

ISBN 13: 978-1-58160-260-9

Printed in the United States of America

Published by Paladin Press, a division of
Paladin Enterprises, Inc.,
Gunbarrel Tech Center
7077 Winchester Circle
Boulder, Colorado 80301 USA
+1.303.443.7250

Direct inquiries and/or orders to the above address.

PALADIN, PALADIN PRESS, and the "horse head" design
are trademarks belonging to Paladin Enterprises and
registered in United States Patent and Trademark Office.

Visit our Web site at www.paladin-press.com

CONTENTS

WARNING

Technical data presented here, particularly technical information on ammunition and the use, adjustment, and alteration of firearms, inevitably reflect the author's beliefs and experience with particular firearms, equipment, and components under specific circumstances which the reader cannot duplicate exactly. The information in this book should therefore be used for guidance only and approached with great caution. Neither the author nor the publisher assumes any responsibility for the use or misuse of information contained in this book.

LYMAN H. POLLOCK, JR.

1925–2000

They earned it.

Thank you, Lyman.

PREFACE

He was the finest man I ever knew. When he died in June of 2000, what I mainly thought of was how lucky I'd been to just meet the man. Without even realizing it, he passed on to me a legacy that cannot be purchased at any price. With a seventh-grade education, he had accomplished more, in real terms, by the time he was 35 than I'll accomplish should I live to be 100. He seldom spoke much of World War II, particularly in his later years.

In 1986, we took my collection of M1s and M14s to Rio Salado range in Mesa, Arizona. It was a crisp, chilly morning such as the desert sometimes provides in April, but when it started to warm up a little, we started to shoot better and enjoy ourselves. He was about 5-foot-6 and weighed perhaps 130 pounds, but I could tell—despite his not having handled one for about 40 years—he regarded my Garands as old friends; he operated them swiftly, efficiently, flawlessly, and very, very fast.

As we were pondering packing up to go, he looked through the spotting scope downrange and saw an unsullied target. He picked up an eight-round clip and smiled, glancing back 100 meters downrange at the target. "Let me show you a little something I learned at Bastogne," he said. "See, we were shooting lot, our shoulders got sore, the Volksies weren't very good shots, so we did this."

I figured "Volksies" referred to the Volksturm Wehrmacht, Hitler's equivalent of the homeguard, and I was still contemplating that when he braced the rifle against his right hip and popped off eight rounds in perhaps five or six seconds.

On the way back from downrange, I held the group thus generated over my chest. All

Wartime Winchester M1 on the hood of a 1942 Jeep with Lyman Pollock's army discharge.

bullets were in the black of the big GI target, scattered over perhaps 8 inches. Not impressive, I thought.

Some years later, with a much better set of Garands, I spent the better part of two days pounding the hell out of my hip bone, trying to equal or exceed Lyman's standard. I never did. I never really got very close. And then came the epiphany.

This was not a skill he had learned casually. And the way he remembered it—complete with all the intricate body and arm movements and alignments—some 40 years later, just for fun, indicated that that this was not a skill he likely used for recreation, either.

He'd told me about "treetoppers" in the Huertgen Forest, German AR234 jets at Remagen, German tanks knocking out 12 to 15 Shermans before P-47s and British Typhoons put them on the run. He'd told me about relieving the German "satellite" camp system and the horrors there. And he'd told me about "bailing out" of half a dozen halftracks, usually because "With a Tiger sitting 25 yards ahead of you, boresighted, and two Panthers ripping down the column beside you, there's nothing else to do!" Most of the stories I doubted, and it wasn't until years later, when I started to read serious history, that it became obvious he was an eyewitness.

I did not doubt his stories for any reason save that his whole demeanor seemed way too "unmilitary" and easygoing, way too funny, entirely unlike John Wayne. His life was simple, straightforward, well ordered, but completely civilized and very civilian. When he left the service, he left it completely. He never attended a 2d or 8th Armored Division reunion, and he wasn't one of those who digs through his medals and decorations periodically as if to verify he was there.

As he faded, I kept thinking of that wonderful line from Spielberg's *Saving Private Ryan*, uttered by the captain as his lifeblood trickled onto the cobblestones: "Earn it." The character in the film, of course, had been saved by his peers, at great cost. But the line, to me, is also about earning a normal life. In the tradition of Cincinnatus, American wartime soldiers have primarily gone back to civilian life with relief. What this generation of men did was earn solid civilian lives and a certain quiet confidence.

Most of America's great heroes, at least among enlisted men, have been those "in for the duration" . . . shoe clerks, plumbers, bartenders, farmers' kids . . . essentially civilians. These men knew the reactionary forces of right-wing fascism had to be met and defeated. Many of the regular soldiers wound up at desk jobs.

Quite by accident, when he visited one day, one of the various Holocaust denial pseudo-historian crackpots was appearing on a cable program, spouting his various fantasies. I could see the look of disgust sneak up, even in the middle of a discussion on a very unrelated subject. "Change the channel, will you? This guy's a liar, and he's making me sick!" So I changed the channel.

Looking back, I realize now why I so

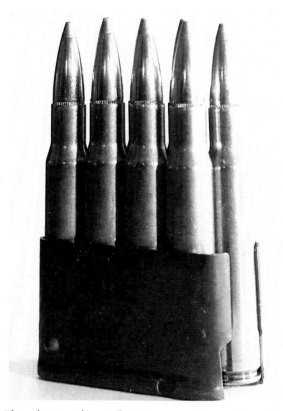

Though viewed as a "flaw" 60 years or more later, the M1's 8-round ejecting clip was really one of its many great strengths.

A rare Breda receiver.

cherish the M1, the Browning Automatic Rifle (BAR), the Thompson submachine gun, even the M1 carbine: We can't retain these men and their vigor, spirit, and stories forever. We can honor what they accomplished, once we understand the real forces involved (the terror, the desperation), but before this book has gone through a couple of printings, many more of them will be gone. This hardware we collect and shoot was American, reliable, powerful, fast. The only full-power, semiautomatic standard infantry rifle in the world, it was conceived by a brilliant Canadian and produced daily by factories in New England, advancing American infantrymen and their tactics into levels of flexibility and mobility far ahead of the rest of the world.

Now, surely, it wasn't just the Ml Garand. More than anything, it was the tough,

resourceful enlisted man, the brilliant amateur who hunkered down and fought like hell and found new ways to make the enemy's life difficult. And in fact, though many editors have, without my permission, inserted George Patton's overblown bombast about the Ml into articles of mine, I have never quoted General Patton in anything in print, and probably not verbally, either. (It's a family thing, you see, for whenever his name came up, remarks about "blood 'n' guts" and things far, far more brutal would reverberate. Many who served in the 2d Armored Division felt that way, and after hearing the ugly stories, so did many of their relatives.)

The Ml, vast numbers of improved radios, many more trucks, half-tracks, better small-unit organization, the incorporation of the BAR

A 2-million range M1 that, ultimately, was restored using parts from Century kits.

A tough old veteran, the author's 1.4 million rifle was visually restored and converted to 7.62x51 NATO with a Springfield match barrel.

Externally, the author's 1.4 million rifle looks as it did during World War II, but it's a modern 7.62 with many parts upgrades.

into every squad and, later, into virtually every front-line fire team, the easy availability of .50-caliber and larger support weapons—every armed force in the world has spun off similar innovations since, but in the period 1939–45, if it was military and American, it worked swiftly. Especially the American fighting man. I cannot afford a Sherman tank or a 105mm howitzer, and I have no place to store either. Currently, I own three M1s, one of them Italian.

It's one of those brilliant, vintage ideas I can constantly upgrade, play with, use to entertain myself, and occasionally do what hardcore collectors do constantly: pose the question,

A rough 'n' tumble 1943 Winchester M1, with a World War II infantryman's memorabilia. This rifle saw tough use, and the blotches on its finish reflect contact with something acid and salt—blood or urine, perhaps?

"What would this thing say if it could talk?" Now, in two cases, I can speculate that one would say, "I spent a lot of time locked in a rifle rack, never getting fired," and another would say, "I was made in Italy and spent about 30 years in Denmark." But the third is a 1.4 million GI Springfield that, when I got it, showed evidence of two wartime rebuilds.

Even if all it saw was lots of training wear, it served, and it served a lot. The Winchester pictured above with my brother-in-law's World War II items shows heavy evidence of a lot of blood on its left side for quite a while. Unlikely it got that way while being stored.

This is a legacy at once simple and immediate and complicated and obscure. I learned from that older generation that freedom is worth fighting for, and even now, I try to do some small thing every day to make this community a little better, to liberate it

some. This isn't easy. On another level, the rifle itself and our firearms rights have to be defended, the M1 in particular.

And don't kid yourself, it's not just liberals attacking us and our hardware. The family that concocted the "Brady" series of calumnies wasn't working for a Democrat when the incident evolved that predicated all this crap. There's a card-carrying Republican conservative former police chief of Los Angeles who doesn't believe in civilian firearms ownership at all. And the former mayor of New York thinks their sort of gun control needs to be exported to the rest of the United States— and trust me, his placards bear a little elephant.

What's happened is very simple. Politicians, left or right, with nothing to offer, need a scapegoat. Hitler did, and the Jews were the first in line. In much of the rest of the world, one cannot publicly persecute

The M1 is one the ultimate service rifles of the 20th century, and very few of its admirers opened their shooting or collecting "careers" with the M1. Not many own just one rifle, either. This is the author's rifle rack, ca. 1992.

minorities by name, though a lot of it goes on implicitly in most of the United States. Hardware is easier, because it isn't human and isn't abstract; you can therefore lie about it without fear of being sued, and even show "frightening" photographs.

Round one of the gun confiscation wars—and that's what we're really fighting now—wasn't lost to Clinton or even in the past couple of decades. It was lost in 1968, when a Senator Thomas Dodd of Connecticut, who was directly on the payroll of several of his home state's firearms manufacturers, confected the Gun Control Act of 1968, which banned all importation of former military firearms, domestic or foreign, into the United States. Dodd was eventually censured by the Senate itself for the various "perks" he received from

the gun manufacturers. An entire generation of "might've been" American gun owners couldn't do what you and I could in the 1960s: mail off $16 to $40 for a nicely made, used former military firearm in good shooting condition, from which to learn things. Only new foreign and U.S.-made firearms were available, and generally at much increased prices. Not only did this not eventuate the economic "boom" the manufacturers anticipated, it precipitated the 1969–86 depression in the firearms industry, from which many firms have never really recovered. Why? Obviously, one develops firearms hobbies—and "hunting" is one of the smallest of that group—by getting in cheap, finding some encouragement, and moving on up if and when one's income increases. The difference between

Someone out there may actually believe that gangbanging idiots shoot the M1, but the fact is that, M1 owners cherish their rifles; crooks are looking for something entirely different.

a 1968 $35 surplus Model 98 Mauser in top condition (a first-class piece of equipment) and a several-hundred-dollar revolver of that vintage (already an antique in concept when made and very possibly defective anyway) as an initial purchase is tremendous. The worst frequency of defective firearms I have ever seen or experienced was with the new guns I handled and tried to shoot in the early 1970s through the mid-1980s; most of the hardware was overpriced, defective junk, and a very high proportion was dangerous to the user.

What Clinton did—and what his successors will try to continue to do—is keep quality goods off the market, not merely to suppress growth in the firearms hobbies and skills, but to enrich the people who pay the bills of corrupt politicians everywhere. Most of the

gun confiscation movement, though it may pretend to have other identities, really has no politics save elitism. And we and our firearms are merely convenient scapegoats.

What we are trying to preserve is a legacy, and not just a legacy of violence, by any means. There's a manufacturing legacy, a design legacy, a service legacy, a training legacy, a shooting legacy—in the end, not much about war, and virtually nothing about crime.

Even if you accept the bland and corrupt presumption that firearms chronically used in crime are particularly worthy of suppression—and I accept that statement only very partially and only in relationship to firearms that are unacceptable to anyone who shoots or collects for recreation—the Ml Garand has seen precious little criminal use. I live in one of those high-crime areas ignored by the local police, and I can tell you for sure that none of the gangbangers and full-time crooks in my area are sitting home tonight indulging fantasies over how badly they'd like to own an M1. Indeed, judging by the looks on their faces when I load mine up to go shooting, they are only vaguely aware that this huge wooden contrivance is a firearm. Now, my Makarov, on the other hand. . . .

I very much doubt that any of my esteemed neighbors could load an M1 without serious injury, and the same is true of most of America's criminal population. But never let it be said that such small nuances have any influence among those who find it convenient to organize to suppress mere machines.

M1 GARAND IN THE 21ST CENTURY

In Mesa, Arizona, where I live, methamphetamine and crack cocaine can be purchased with slightly greater ease than a cup of coffee or a pack of cigarettes, and the local police—who persist in claiming they need many more officers—send five to seven cars to minor traffic episodes in certain neighborhoods. They don't do what used to be called "law enforcement" in most of the city; it would interfere with their public relations efforts and confuse the city's "founders," who witlessly recite the old refrain about what a wonderful, happy town it is.

But never fear! Ml receivers can no longer be imported into the United States! Therefore, we are all safe! This logic may seem a little muddy to some of us, particularly to me, since I wound up going all the way to trial for assault after being attacked by three local gangbangers in an incident where *only I* got injured. But that's what happens when lowlifes and lunatics make the rules, essentially running the asylum. (The jury saw through several bits of perjury and fraud, and the verdict was "innocent" . . . after I'd wasted many thousands of dollars on an incident that, in a rational place, never would have even resulted in an arrest.) The relationship between the issues? What it is, in both cases, is the triumph of the sleazoid crackpots.

Very quietly, the United States—primarily since the end of the Cold War—has slipped into a prosecutorial justice system in which most people are guilty until proven innocent. Rules, conversations, and whole segments of public and private discourse no longer even resemble the rational interchange of years past. It isn't freedoms we're losing—it's *sanity*!

For some 20 years now, I've avoided politics in general, particularly at the dirty local level, and especially here in Arizona. No longer. I am thrice burned and many times wise. That is what the last generation taught me: when you see insanity and injustice being sold like soap, whichever side of the political spectrum it comes from, it has to be fought! The Y2K scam, bogus multilevel money swap plans, the conspiracy theory of more or less everything, Maricopa County's bogus "justice" system . . . they get tedious because all they amount to is somebody's lunatic fringe profit-making business. But the Ml receiver ban? Ah, there it is, in a nutshell! The perfect solution for which there was no problem—and never has been! Hopefully, this ban will be reversed sometime soon.

In the meantime, there is no silver lining, but there are some rays of sunlight emerging through the clouds.

A Harrington & Richardson (H & R) being fired. The M1 is a rifle requiring discipline and some knowledge.

The author test-fires a postwar M1.

PARTS AND STARTS

There aren't a great many M1 rifles floating around the world now. But when the Danish military recently decided to dispose of its stocks of Garands, some were returned via Military Aid Program channels and sold through the Civilian Marksmanship Program. These were the very receivers we gave the Danes under NATO and other Mutual Defense Pacts from 1949 onward. The remainder—Berettas, Bredas, and open-market U.S.-built rifles purchased from third countries—was sold to Century Arms, a Canadian company with headquarters in Florida and Vermont. But the ban dictated that the receivers were stuck in Canada, off Century's purchase, so several thousand parts kits were made available in the United States at rather attractive prices. A few

receivers dribbled south, and some came in just before the ban, but, for the most part, there are vast numbers of parts and very few receivers. (Both receivers and parts will be discussed later, in more detail.)

Not to allow the surfeit of parts to go unexploited, Illinois-based Springfield Armory, Incorporated announced that it planned on reentering the receiver market with its investment cast receiver by December 2000. IAI, the Israeli manufacturer, will produce a receiver in this country fairly soon, adding to its product line, which already includes a very high-quality M1 carbine receiver. Entréprisé Arms has shown its prototype and has been advertising its new units since 1998 or so. Century Arms, in possession of most of the parts kits, engaged a firm in Spain to produce castings, which were then machined and finished in this country by Caspian Arms, which produced many parts for the Model 1911 pistol. Later receivers will be cast in this country and machined and finished by Ruger. As of now, only complete rifles are leaving Century, and they'll be analyzed in this tome based on my tests. Later, receivers will be available separately.

The old standbys of the wood business, Fajen and Bishop, were both purchased by Missouri reloading supplier Midway Arms and basically liquidated. Some Fajen and Bishop products may appear occasionally, but since the tools and assets of the firms were sold, these will be made elsewhere. Therefore virtually the only quantity supplier of Garand stocks—brand new civilian ones that can be counted on to fit and work—is Boyd's. Some Italian stocks of rather nice quality have entered the country, and the same fiberglass units available in 1992 are still in production.

Barnett, Wilson, Obermeyer, and some others are producing M1 barrels, and many brands of blanks are being reconfigured to fit the M1. I acquired two of Fulton Armory's standard barrels to test for this book, the results of which are included. What it all boils down to is that, despite efforts to kill it off by the fools who continually try to rain on every parade they do not understand, the Garand is alive, well, and getting better in the 21st century.

BMF, which designed and produced the straightpull conversion kit for the M1, seems to be completely gone. I tried to locate the firm via every search engine and technique, and though I found several firms using the same initials, none had anything to do with firearms, let alone the M1 Garand. Too bad. Everything that increases the Garand's versatility increases its life. And the more enthusiasts we can recruit and keep active, the longer all of us—collectors, shooters, and tinkerers—can look forward to having the material around.

Since 1992, several manufacturers have introduced kits for molycoating bullets (the process has been somewhat streamlined), and, perhaps most important of all, Sierra has introduced several precision-coated bullets in its standard line. Using its bullets primarily, I have not had *any* evidence of the periodic flyers many people seem to experience with molycoated bullets.

As I predicted, more high-quality .308/7.62 NATO ammo has reached the market, though somewhat surprisingly, the remanufactured .30/06 on Lake City brass is still around in sizable lots. But for the shooter, there is *still* great advantage in setting up a recreation or competition rifle in the newer, shorter cartridge.

We'll also do more in the way of working information for the M1 bolt stripdown, the ejector-extractor-firing pin work attendant to making the rifle work a little slicker than its military incarnation, and we'll discuss an almost foolproof trigger job technique. Remember I said "almost" foolproof: some fool will exaggerate something and ruin it, so what this one does is engineer problems out for all but the clumsiest and stupidest, against whom there is ultimately *no* protection.

And, much against my better judgment, I've finally included a date chart, with some detail. I adapted it from eight or 10 sources and took out most of the things that are very controversial. If you need more detail, read Scott Duff's books.

I'm trying to set you up to use, admire, and collect the M1 Garand, and to avoid a lot of problems. The main thing, though, is to appreciate this machine and its legacy.

Citadel, the barrel maker, is gone. Its "run-of-the-mill" merchandise was highly variable, but its very best was superb. I ran an exhaustive test (which isn't included because you can't get the product), and I got definitive news of final collapse after having just spent the several hundred bucks on ammo and shot it for the test!

The detailed parts photos are designed to explain and illustrate a great deal that appeared in the earlier volume and that may have passed by too quickly. And I'm including accessory information, though not much of it.

You may recall, I said in *The Complete M1 Garand* that I had not seen a Breda receiver and wouldn't be surprised if there were none. Well,

I'll show and examine that and some other Italian variations. And I will discuss and more or less dismiss the "flaws" in the M1, including some that have never been publicly explored before. I mean this book to be practical, with lots of nuts and bolts. And this time, I'll assert myself.

The main thing is enjoyment. For despite the fact that Mr. Garand's machine was intended for military use, its main strength was not "killing people," which is a tiny part of what even military arms do; its main strength was and is that it's fun to use. Perhaps that's why it performed so well 55 to 60 years ago (as this is written), in the hands of the golden amateurs who saved the world.

PART 1

THE ONGOING HISTORY
OF THE M1 GARAND

The Complete M1 Garand was designed from the outset to be the first single book to address the M1 as a shooting machine, collector's item, and artifact, in a volume directed to the reloader, technician, competition shooter, and perhaps even a kid contemplating purchasing the old war horse. In the past, there were books for collectors, books for shooters, manuals, and technical/mechanical books, none of which had enough overlap to automatically be applicable for everyone who enjoys the M1.

But the history of the rifle didn't end in 1957 or even in 1992. The gun confiscation lobby *wants* to end that long parade, much as it wants to end the history of firearms in general, at least among people who are not wealthy, and an elitist calumny that the M1 is "ideal for gangbangers" has resulted in a ban upon the further civilian importation of the M1. Other than the patently obvious fact that people who say such ridiculous things have never lived in the ghetto (which I have and do), where mechanisms with the bulk and weight of the Garand are regarded with looks of absolute bafflement, such fantasies demonstrate how "targeting" and "scapegoating" work for the forces of elitism. As well, the currencies of exchange in the cutthroat world of the crack dealer, the speed freak, the burglar, the casual criminal, and the lower elements of disorganized crime are chemical, legal tender, and cheap or stolen handguns and large-magazine short guns of much smaller dimensions. If there's ever been a low-level armed robbery or drive-by shooting with an M1 Garand, it's buried very deep in somebody's

records. Not, mind you, that facts, logic, and truth mean anything to the elitists who, when the rest of us have been disarmed, will still be able to afford cadres of gun-wielding goons.

The M1 is the most popular high-powered target semiautomatic in the world, and probably the strongest. It is also the last actual issue U.S. military rifle that can be owned by a

The M1 is a rifle that can tear up a digit, and it requires some background in mechanical principles to operate properly. Even loading clips is beyond the capability of many crooks, and getting them into the rifle would remain a puzzlement.

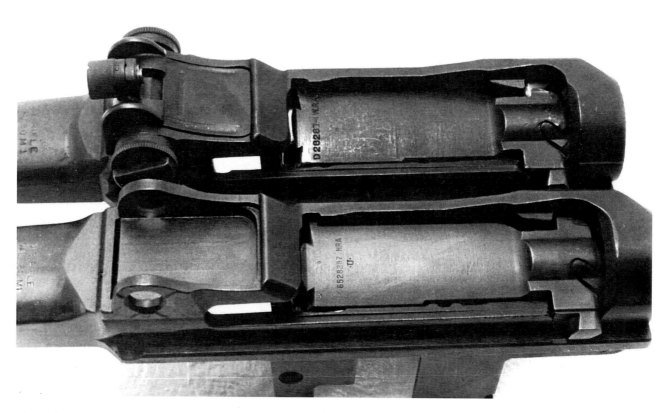

The early Winchester receiver (top), fitted with a National Match rear sight and correct bolt, and the H&R (bottom) are quite different. Some collectors think the strange extra projection right in front of the left bolt lug might have once been to secure early type of receivers in some kind of fixture. The improved and thicker "horseshoe" aft of the rear sight area on the H&R is also visible and obvious. This rifle is still evolving.

civilian without the financial and paperwork nightmares of an National Firearms Act (NFA)-registerable receiver.

Much against my better judgment—because such items are frequently thought of as chapter and verse—I am including in Chapter 5 date charts and guidelines for U.S.-produced M1 rifles, emphasizing World War II production. These are guides *only* and must be treated as such. The notes in the charts, drawn from Garand Collectors Association (GCA) documentation, Duff, dozens of other sources, and my own research on the rifles themselves, are probably more important than the dates themselves. Firearms, especially during World War II, were not built to please collectors or fill logbooks; barrels available were put on receivers as available, and sometimes even major changes in production did not arrive "kerbam" on one particular serial number. More important is the general production pattern, very

simply expressed by the real rule of the M1's production life: from inception to the end of military forged-receiver production, everything got better. The difference between a -2 receiver of 1940–41 and a -35 of 1945 is profound.

The difference in quality of detail fit and finish between, say, 1942 and 1955 is at least as great.

Thanks to the importation of considerable numbers of parts kits and a few more receivers, we now know a great deal more about Italian production in general, and the Danish lots in particular. It is unlikely that we'll ever know everything about Italian M1 production and markings, since these guns were ordered in many small variants and permutations of marking and numbering, but it is now possible to detail Breda production and accurately show Danish receiver markings, both of which I at one time thought might be fictional.

CHAPTER 1
THE TACTICAL HISTORY OF THE M1 GARAND: SOME THOUGHTS, RECOLLECTIONS, AND ANALYSIS

The "fire-and-maneuver" tactics that made the World War II American infantry unit so formidable evolved in direct response to the nightmare of World War I. Many traditionalists in the military had opposed all the changes necessary to institute these new concepts and, ironically, some of those people wound up benefiting from the new concepts of movement, fire base, communications, and logistics.

All the competing designs in the development of the M1—and the M1 itself—were designed around a new family of 7mm cartridges similar to the concepts, originally British, intended for the Pattern 13 and, in turn, similar to the .280 Ross. These cartridges featured faster burning powders, excellent accuracy, high orders of sectional density, and somewhat reduced muzzle blast and recoil. (Copper fouling, however, would have been a problem.) Early on, the radicals behind all this activity envisioned, as well, all-tracked infantry and support; radios and communications gear everywhere; and everything fast, flexible, and efficient.

The American military, from 1919 to 1941, was comparatively tiny. But despite the calls for isolationism emanating from the American right wing, by 1923 any rational analyst of world affairs knew there would be another "big one," most likely covering two oceans and, therefore, much bigger than the last one. The services and designers toiled quietly and on a shoestring until the Great Depression sucked the life and the money out of virtually all but the smallest development programs.

Revisionist historians often like to mull over how much "better off" the United States might have been had more money been directed to the military during the Depression, rather than toward civilian programs, but the facts and the hardware involved would have meant that by the time we entered the war in late 1941 we'd have had vast quantities of inappropriately trained personnel and obsolete, expensive equipment quite incapable of fighting the real war. Masses of P-26, P-36, and P-40 fighter planes to fight the war of the 1940s might have inspired confidence somewhere, but the simple truth is that new designs just coming off drawing boards were what was needed, and had a huge inventory of the earlier hardware been purchased already, the long-term effect would have been to set back the progressive programs that actually mattered. For example, despite the fact that leading-edge tank designs that originated here were developed elsewhere, the armored vehicles our government could have acquired early would have been obsolete by 1940 and the United States simply could not spend the money for capital-intense durable goods, and dared not spend on the sinkhole of dead-end military goods. America's wounds from the Great Depression required healing, and priorities were in directions other than military monuments, and for pressing reasons which, short-term, relegated military equipment needs to prudent planning.

But the smaller programs could be advanced and financed. Tactics could be developed, and foreign tactics could be studied, adapted, and refined. U.S. industrial power was part dormant in the 1930s, with our labor force in a desperate struggle for survival. The economy improved in fits and starts from 1933, and civilian demand—far more productive and constructive than

The M1903 Springfield (basically a modified M98 Mauser) was the M1's service predecessor. Although an excellent rifle, it couldn't even compare in World War II firepower terms, and after World War II it was found to not be as inherently accurate, either, in anything like service or standard match form.

military spending—gradually rose. But increases in military spending were few until 1940. The fire-and-maneuver concept was straightforward, and it called upon skills still fairly common in the United States: the rifle and the rifleman were the basic unit of advance, with all other personnel and devices serving as support. We had the other weapons: the BAR, the Browning .30s in the weapons units, the Browning .50s at a higher level. But the bolt-action rifle—and it didn't matter which bolt-action rifle—simply couldn't be operated quickly and efficiently enough to spread firepower delivery down the chain reliably.

There are those who dispute this. A British marine once explained to me in depth that he had participated in a firepower demonstration during which his unit, using No. 4 Mk 1 Enfield rifles in .303, had "out-shot" American personnel with M1s. Although he was telling the truth and had the photos and targets to prove it, that was a very special case. Bear in mind that the Enfields carry 10 rounds. This was the early 1950s, and most of his team comprised NCOs—tough, experienced World War II veterans—who'd been firing those rifles for seven to 10 years. The Americans were mainly recent draftees.

Every British rifle was brand new or freshly rebuilt, whereas the American rifles were of varying qualities and vintages and had been in Germany since the end of World War II. And yet, the scores were quite close, with the U.S. GIs generating slightly more bull's-eyes, which

British Enfield No. 4 Mk 1 rifles such as the British sometimes claimed could "outshoot" the M1 . . . and under sufficiently unusual and contrived conditions, they probably could!

was more than offset by a number of rounds in the white or off the paper entirely. And of course, there was a factor I've noticed in shooting both rifles myself: in rapid fire, the British rifle, more so than the M1, generally trails off in accuracy due to heat buildup after about 15 rounds. And as an observer of this same demonstration remarked, the various hand and shoulder movements involved in operating the bolt-action rifles made their shooters much more visible at range. Most people seem to agree that the amount of training required to deliver rapid fire accurately with most any semiautomatic rifle is far less than with bolt actions of any type or design. In short, the exercise was a wonderful demonstration of what the very best training and experience can deliver with one weapon, but the other competitor proved quite capable of delivering similar results with far less specialized preparation.

Bear in mind that military bolt-action rifles had been around for 60-odd years, and the Enfield system itself for more than 50, when this "comparison" took place and was apparently repeated at NATO bases all over Europe. The gas port version of the M1 was less than 15 years old, and, though well developed, many of the rifles involved bore original barrels at least 10 years old.

Much of American military thinking had been bound to mechanisms similar to the bolt action. It was said that semiautomatics would greatly increase ammunition demand. This was correct, but logistics improvements provided plenty of ammo. It was said that troops would relax fire discipline on the theory that anything missed on the first round could be hit with the next. "Experts" recalled the Mondragon and various Mauser and other full-powered semiautomatics, dismissing them as "fragile," "erratic," "inaccurate," and "purely specialist's weapons." Those actually in the firearms industry, which also experienced the Depression at its worst, stepped forward to advise that they already had various designs.

In the period 1964–67, I was already an M1 owner and shooter. I sought out veterans and armorers and, when possible, pumped them for information. Using the microfilm resources of my university library and twice even venturing to the Library of Congress, I meticulously dug through mass-media and specialized sporting/shooting publications for references to what was already my favorite rifle. With the rifles I actually owned and fired, I found it difficult to rationalize much of the exposure that the M1 received up to about 1941. Generally scathingly negative, and never very specific, there were references to inaccuracy and unreliability and even inferences of catastrophic failure. I copied and transcribed and compared, and noted with

some confusion that very little "official" literature seemed to confirm or even address these matters. And I was baffled that none of the mass-media coverage included *any* mention of the new tactical developments. Obviously, this was not my entire life, but being relentless in general and inquisitive by nature, I asked the smiths of my acquaintance for information. And I got it.

Jake wasn't real jolly, and he could be very uncommunicative, but when he communicated, it was in short sentences and very clear: "Combination of hogwash and little bits of truth!" He snatched an odd-looking, dusty M1 off the rack from among his eight or 10 Garands, and I immediately noticed its squared-off gas cylinder and muzzle apparatus and its four-digit serial number. We wiped it off and talked as he secured it in his vise fixtures and began to remove the gas cylinder, which was nothing I'd seen before on an M1, though I dimly recognized the blocky part. "See the funny rubbed spot here?" he asked, pointing to a shiny spot about one-third of the way back along the receiver's operating rod raceway.

"Well, rubbing there, especially if you didn't load clips with the first—and therefore, the *last*—round to the right, along with some other little glitches, would freeze the @®Ù#@ action on the seventh round." He finally screwed the gas cylinder off, and I noticed that the barrel was shorter than mine was. He exposed the "gas trap" blast cone. "This damned thing probably woulda worked okay with new .276 ammo with faster powders, but it was a #®Ù@&*& nightmare with .30 caliber, especially match ammo and old stuff!" (He would explain more afterward, which I'll cover later.) He meticulously cleaned the interior of the gas cylinder before putting the rifle back on the rack. "I can't replace that gas cylinder, and I never shoot that gun—not since '40, anyway. It's really a prototype, and it's the first M1 I ever shot much. So it might be valuable someday." It would be almost 20 years before I saw another gas trap M1, though oddly, I'd seen some of the old gas cylinders in store at a nearby army base, and I didn't, until that moment, have the vaguest idea what they were for.

"See, the military don't like to change nothin'! And anytime anything does change, there's always some $#@&Ù®Ç who wants to make lots of money off it, and he's always got some better way to do this, that, or the other thing! Sure, it always works better, he's had it layin' around for years, that other idea is stupid, and, by the way, did he mention, it also costs a helluva lot less?"

I still didn't quite comprehend his meaning.

"Didja ever wonder why all this nasty crap about the M1 stopped more or less the very *day* Winchester got the private contract? Whole bunch o' businesses wanted government work, so they'd plant stories—any damned thing, long as it was partways true—and that's why every little glitch or wrinkle with anything new got made into a catastrophe, whereas if some o' their crap *#&%$#' *exploded*, well, hell, that's somebody else's fault!"

COMBAT

Fire and maneuver was the very opposite of the Continental European concept of the automatic base of fire, wherein the machine gun is primary and everything else support, but it, very simply, spreads firepower and encourages aggressive movement at much lower levels. In fact, the Japanese concept was similar to ours but so heavily steeped in errant philosophy that tactical instrumentation was much different. Yet the Japanese were studying and attempting to copy the Garand—apparently based on procured rifles and/or stolen blueprints—very early on.

The M1 ejects its flimsy sheet-metal clip at the end of eight rounds, and the distinct "ping" was sometimes viewed as a disadvantage. Some World War II veterans claimed they'd toss an empty clip to the ground after a couple of rounds just in case the enemy might take this as a reloading signal, but I've been told by at least two veterans that no one reacted at all. Perhaps enemy soldiers never heard the sound, or perhaps they were unwilling to take what would have been a terminal chance to show themselves or break cover. But clips of eight rounds, quickly replenished, in the hands of a well-trained squad supported by at least one BAR is a great deal of full-house firepower, quite capable of suppressing movement out to 1,000 meters with no further support. The rhythm and rapidity of fire, all by itself, will keep an enemy formation ducking and dodging, and therefore movement forward becomes a possibility. This is not to say that a German formation could not do the same, but it created much more of its entire density of fire from its one or two machine guns, which were also much more easily located. The percentage of fire delivered by the machine guns was far higher. Taking out the machine gun or its crew, obscuring the automatics' fields of fire, avoiding the main source of bulk firepower . . . these were more easily refined for use against such formations than against American units.

But, of course, this massing of fire *suggests* something similar to area or volley fire, and the traditional military shooting technique has always called for firing *only* when a specific target is in the sights. This controversy predates the M1 by centuries, but in the 20th century numerous rifles had become available that could kill easily at 1,000 meters and beyond. In particular, the U.S. Marine Corps opposed the change in fire concept originally and expressed no interest in the M1; not too long thereafter, it became their "baby," and though the training did not change very much, in the field, covering and suppressive fire—in tremendous volume—became as effective as the British, decades earlier, had hoped their "grid volley fire" might be. The M1 could never spray down the landscape like a submachine gun or the German MG42, but especially working in groups, from good cover, there was minimal body movement required to fire and reload, and in terms of rounds or power, well-trained men, especially men who trained together and knew each other, could move against far superior numbers with some alacrity.

There are no panaceas. Nothing is perfect. But while the difference between one man with a Pattern 17 Enfield or M1903 Springfield and

Early on, the M1 carbine wasn't directly incorporated into standard infantry units but wound up being the standard weapon for anyone who had other support duties—radiomen, assistant BAR men, officers, and sometimes NCOs. This, though, is a later M2 carbine, which by the time of the Korean War had been neatly folded into a fire-and-maneuver tactical package.

one with an M1 is fairly substantial, the difference between an experienced squad with bolt-action rifles and an experienced squad with M1s (presuming similar support) is rather astounding. The Germans, the Soviets, and the British all admired the increased American firepower delivery system and eventually used different solutions to achieve similar results in some selected units, or merely added submachine guns to increase the number of rounds fired by most units. But only the United States could boast full-power, high-outflow, long-range weaponry in every combat unit after the middle of 1942.

I have interviewed enough German and Japanese veterans of that conflict to know that the fascist enemies were fully aware of this.

CHAPTER 2
THE INDUSTRIAL AND DEVELOPMENTAL HISTORY OF THE M1 GARAND

The '03 Springfield was essentially a Model 98 Mauser slightly modified from the original German design to suit American tooling and manufacturing techniques, and with sights specified by U.S. Ordnance officials. The Pattern 17 Enfield was very similar, but a British design simply adapted to the American .30-06 round. Their predecessor, the Krag, was a very traditional Danish/Norwegian design, again adapted to American sight preferences, with the caliber changed. The old Model 1873 Springfield and its various successor and spin-off single-shot rifles were straightforward developments of very traditional caplock designs. In short, until the Garand came along, American military long arms were not very innovative and demanded minimal tooling and manufacture research.

Springfield Armory, however, had developed much of the industrial discipline associated with mass production and interchangeable parts, and, indeed, the large-scale machine production of finished products was frequently referred to as "armory procedure." Much later, Henry Ford became closely associated with the "assembly line," and the 19th-century accomplishments of the mother armory in Massachusetts were largely forgotten.

The Garand demanded some fairly subtle contouring and milling, and the specification was upgraded virtually continuously from about 1932 until 1945 and, much more gradually, even in the 1952–57 period. Many of these small permutations were covered photographically in *The Complete M1 Garand*, and it seems that some

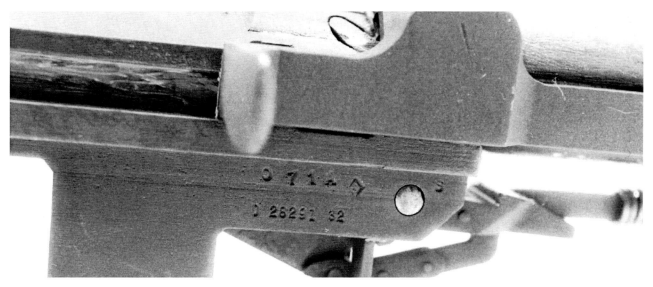

Much of the Garand's contouring, fitting, and, most important, true parts interchange depended on the strict application of what was called "armory procedure," which meant leaving encoded tracks of heat treatment, drawing number, steel manufacturers, and the like on major parts, such as the cryptic notations on this 1944 -32 receiver.

of the various contour changes had to do, perhaps, with fixtures or jigs intended to secure the receiver during test or manufacture.

Duff's comprehensive volumes include far more in the way of detail than we have room for here. His research was primarily done at Springfield Armory and is found in official military records. But there are some general observations that are productive in analyzing this great rifle's long, successful history.

Perhaps the most significant single change was quite early, ca. 1941–42, when the base specification was rewritten to call out 8620 steel, rather than the traditional "41" series ordnance steel. This steel had been used in some firearms applications before, but it was mainly thought of as a tool and spring material. When the hardness and heat-treatment specifications—which were rigorously followed at Springfield Armory and not so rigorously at Winchester—were changed in approximately 1943, the receiver had reached a point of optimum strength that remained basically unchanged in receivers of similar design through the Beretta BM series and the American M14.

All military M1s were produced from pressure forgings. With some exceptions, all civilian receivers have been produced from investment castings. Simply put, the difference between the two is bubbles—and therefore strength. Forgings are essentially crushed while hot and thus compressed to an approximation of the necessary shape. Castings are simply poured. Forgings are somewhat denser, albeit careful heat treatment can make up for some of the differences in strength. And the M1, like most products of its time, was considerably overbuilt. Still, no cast M1 or M14 or "M1A" receiver can truly be called "Mil Spec," because the first specification page begins, "Forging shall be of 8620 steel, heat treated. . . ."

Incidentally, I have seen the original drawing file on the M14 at Smith Enterprises (then in Mesa, Arizona, now in Tempe), and much of the M1 file as well. These documents, though in the public domain, constitute a vast file—weighing well over 130 pounds for the M1 alone—and

describe precisely the manufacture in detail of each part. The attendant documents and orders at least equal the drawings in volume.

Smith has produced *forged* M14 receivers, and after long consultation and actual observation of the manufacturing process, I inquired, "Isn't the M14 kind of a 1930s-style creature?" The answer was real simple: "Yes!" But some parenthetical data were immediately added. On both the M1 and the M14, the manufacturing baseline can be achieved with CNC (Computer Numerically Controlled) machinery, though many smaller items can be wholly manufactured using CNC and other more modern techniques. Still, the final fitting, contouring, and prefinishing detail is done by hand, measuring, filing, buffing, inspecting, measuring again, and so on, because the manner in which the receiver interacts with other attendant parts is quite subtle. No matter what, the manufacture of an M1 receiver is virtually the same process, even though the operating rod and various other parts are significantly different. The M1 was also the first American military rifle to employ stainless steel, primarily the gas cylinder itself and the

The stainless-steel gas cylinder of the M1 led to various letter-coded experiments to get better finish adhesion, few of which have ever been deciphered, but which eventually led to far more durable finish methods.

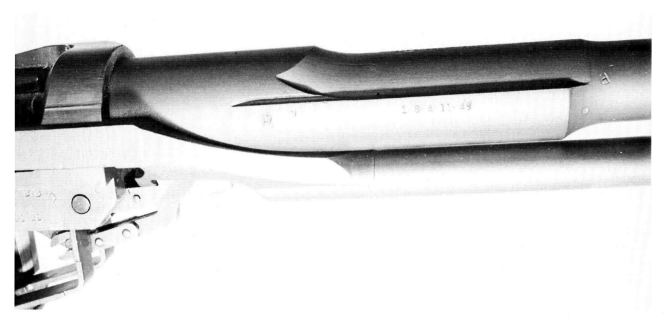

Original November 1943 barrel, marked in the definitive (but not ubiquitous) World War II manner. Markings evolved for the convenience of armorers, not collectors.

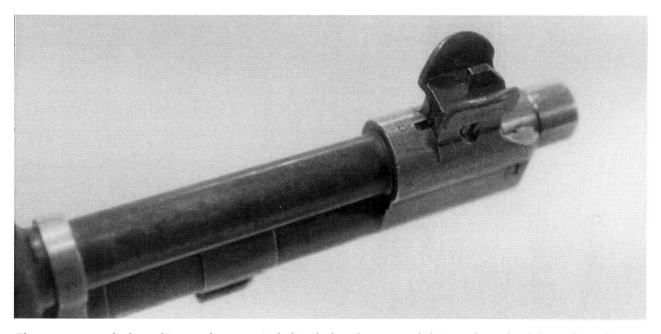

The gas trap gas cylinder and its attendant parts, including the barrel, cannot truly be interchanged with later rifles in the normally understood sense of the word.

gas piston on the operating rod. Getting the finish on this material to last proved to be elusive, which is why so many "gas port" cylinders bear small, cryptic letters. Finish experiments were conducted at the armory almost constantly until at least 1948, and, of course, no "perfect" solution was ever found, which is why so many gas cylinders today are shiny bright. Oxides, which were far better than the early "pickling" processes, went on the last issues, but the ultimate answer was to have the cylinders refinished regularly. Most collectors

The follower arm of the M1 improved in strength but became more difficult to mount and dismount, with the "long fork" version on the top, compared to a riveted "short fork," ca.1942–43, below. To shooters, there's no functional difference.

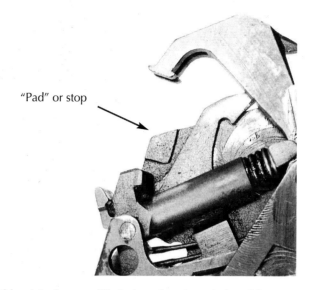

"Pad" or stop

Old, original, unmodified trigger housings designed for "flat-top" safeties whose stop pads have never been reconfigured, such as this one, will not function with the much more common "round-top" improved safeties.

and shooters have found that applications of automotive high-temperature engine paints or charcoal-grill paint will keep the surface satisfactorily matte without detracting from the rifle's looks, and in fact many of us use this same stuff on other small, nonmoving parts, especially buttplates, and then bake it on. This isn't faking or chicanery; it's practical corrosion prevention and glare reduction.

Generally, every part on the M1 rifle got continuously better. Extraneous machining operations were eliminated, oddments of excessive contouring disappeared, and the receiver got stronger, along with virtually every other part of the rifle. While it's generally correct to say that virtually every M1 Garand part can be interchanged with every other M1, there are two exceptions—one very obvious, the other slightly more subtle. First, neither the barrel proper nor the gas cylinder and attendant front sight assembly of the "gas trap" rifles can be interchanged with later units, though it would be theoretically possible to put the *entire* gas trap apparatus intact on more or less any M1—barrel, cylinder, sights, all subordinate front end parts. The other one—which I had forgotten about until I ran into the CMP rifle whose trigger assembly appears here—is one we don't think about much until we actually encounter the parts combination: the original trigger housings, up until 1941 (and much later at Winchester), utilized a larger "stop" machined in for the older, weaker "flat-top" safety. A "flat-top" safety can be used in any trigger housing, though collectors and shooters would both want *not* to do so, but the newer *safeties will not fit the original trigger housings with unmodified stops.* Because of their value, of course, such trigger housings should not be modified; they should be sold or traded or used with original flat safeties, but *never* remachined.

The photographs here examine some parts development—the "extra rail" configuration receivers, a few contour permutations, and so on.

Again, I want to stress this: as in the rest of the shooting sports, it is more imperative than ever that shooters and collectors come together, not just to present a "united front" to the gun confiscation lobby, but to help each other in day-to-day events, restorations, and shooting events.

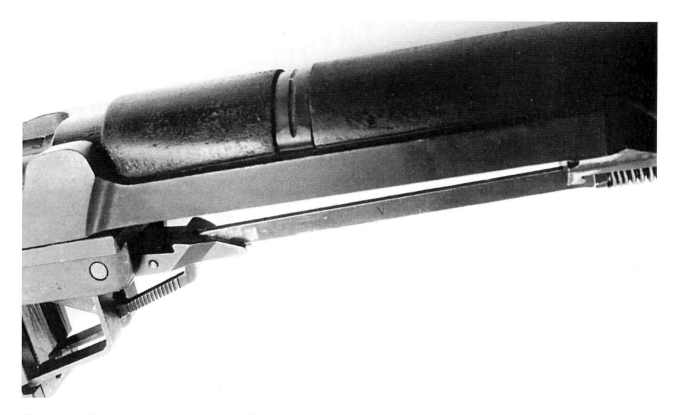

Though Winchester's output of M1s was smaller than Springfield's (this is Winchester's very first rifle, 100001), Winchester never incorporated many of the changes that were almost constant at the Springfield Armory, and this 1940 WRA isn't much different from a rifle of five years later.

Closeup of the Winchester buttplate. Note the distinct "border" around flat-ended "checkering."

The Winchester bayonet lugs do not have the frontal "toe" of all other M1's *unless* one has been beaten, milled, or filed over the years by someone.

CHAPTER 3
NEW M1S FOR THE 21ST CENTURY: THE DANISH KITS AND BEYOND

For about two years at the time of this writing, Century Arms, the Canadian-owned firm with offices in Vermont and Florida, has been importing parts kits of M1s, complete except for receivers. Apparently there were originally just over 20,000 rifles that formed the base of this group, of which Century was the main importer.

Denmark returned the lion's share of those it had received free of charge under MAP to the U.S. government, in accordance with the original agreement. These, in turn, were made available through the CMP to qualified purchasers as complete rifles. However, the receivers Century purchased mostly stayed in Canada. This glut of parts spurred more domestic receiver production, which will be discussed separately. A few complete rifles trickled into the United States by various means before the ban on importation of the Garand receiver took effect.

Denmark's long association with the North Atlantic Treaty Organization (NATO) and participation in exercises with U.S. troops meant its armament took on a quite cosmopolitan inventory. Since NATO members generally were required to issue arms in NATO caliber from the early 1950s, many collectors had presumed that M1s in stock would have been converted predominantly to the 7.62x51 chambering made standard in 1953–55. But this proved not to be the case.

THE PARTS

Long before this book was in the works, I contacted Steve Kehaya at Century Arms to begin obtaining parts kits and information. Until recent "musical chairs" began in the editorial offices of the many firearms magazines for which I used to write, it was my custom to generate two to five M1 articles annually as updates. And I found it possible to squirrel away some decent M1 receivers for future projects, which, as of late 1998 or so, were sitting around gathering dust.

There is a vast economic difference between buying individual parts and getting everything in a kit. As this is being written, complete M1 kits can be had from $125 to just short of $200. A decent barrel, all by itself, will get into these price ranges wholesale, and an operating rod will run $35 to $100. Bolts? $20 to $60! Add the small parts, pins, wood . . . purchased individually, the parts can cost $500 or more.

The 15 or so kits I purchased made obvious the Danish acquisition pattern, which was later corroborated by other collectors. Most of their U.S.-made M1s were acquired in the early 1950s. By the middle to late 1950s, rifles from Italy, with the unique Danish markings shown on the next page, were being purchased new. And, apparently, quite a few were purchased well into the 1960s from third-party countries or U.S. inventories, separately from the MAP acquisitions. I made a point of going through parts purchased by other M1 buffs, and what I found basically confirmed this information.

The Danes seem to have manufactured two major parts only: barrels and buttstocks. The barrels bore the same proofs that rifle and machine gun buffs had noted on fine Madsen

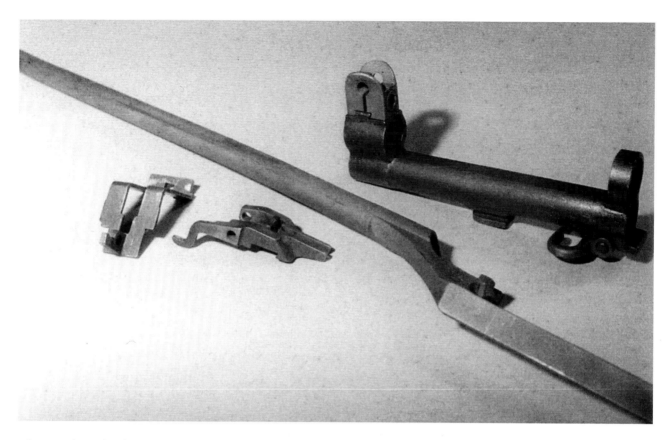

The Danish M1 kits from Century provided a great many high-quality parts. All gas cylinders, operating rods, and other moving parts, such as the operating rod catch and bullets guides, bolts, and so on proved to be of very high quality.

The Danish-made beech stocks were nicely fitted and very sturdy. Virtually all the M1 buttstocks from Denmark carried the receiver's serial numbers ahead of the rear sling swivel.

arms for years and were mainly from the late 1950s and early 1960s. The wood made in Denmark was European beech, strangely reminiscent of the K98k of a generation earlier, but closely cut and well made and surely prettier than the American birch stocks.

Danish stocks were generally stamped with the serial number of the receiver just ahead of

Some of the early parts in the Danish kits made it possible to restore receivers that had been sitting for some time, such as these three, to complete working condition. Note the extra "guide rail" ahead of the follower grooves on the center receiver, which some collectors think might be for an accessory never actually introduced or for some kind of production fixture that did not stay in use for long.

the butt sling swivel, sometimes adjacent to the receiver heel, and many stocks had been drilled and countersunk for what must have been British-style unit ID discs, most commonly in the "heel" of the pistol grip. This was done on American- and Italian-produced wood as well, though most commonly on the beech units. These serial numbers allowed some conclusions to be drawn about the times and nature of service lots.

Most numbers manufactured were well below the 3.8–3.9 million figure generally thought of as very late World War II production. A lot of four-digit numbers suggested Italian rifles, and usually these were with kits including Beretta and Breda parts. I have not yet seen—and I've gone through at least 25 kits—a number over 4.2 million and have seen perhaps half a dozen American parts associated with U.S.-built rifles after 1952. To

enumerate: one International Harvester (IHC) hammer, one 65 series Springfield operating rod, one H&R hammer, one postwar Springfield Armory (SA) bolt, and a safety.

A considerable number of "type 3" sights and D35382 relieved operating rods from the immediate postwar period, mixed with a fairly high percentage of "locking bar" rear sights, suggested shipment of a lot of unmodified and/or once-rebuilt World War II U.S. rifles.

I retrieved a wealth of World War II parts, however—some of them very hard to find and quite valuable. I was, in fact, able to build up a 3.3 million rifle, with an approximately correct barrel and stock, by careful sifting. Also found and worthy of mention: a near-mint, uncut WRA operating rod, a complete set of very early Springfield bands and operating rod catch, several very early bolts, and lots of early gas cylinders. I observed only two World War

Not many Winchester barrels were among the Danish kits, though this one, which belonged to a collector, was in virtually perfect condition, all by itself worth more than he paid for the entire kit.

Breda barrels were quite common in the shipments from Denmark via Century. This one was apparently built by Beretta to service a Breda rifle, as it also carries the B.SID notation generic to Breda M1s.

II Springfield barrels but many replacements, ca. 1947–52.

The Danish barrels showed signs of very high quality, and I found several Breda barrels, which I had never seen before. I would later find myself shooting a Danish barrel on one of Century's receivers, now *finally* (effective July 2000) available separately, and that experience would confirm my measurements and observations.

All of the Danish parts were in at least solid condition, most were excellent, and I did not

Typical Danish-made barrel, of very high quality.

encounter a barrel whose throat erosion gauge reading was worse than 3.5. And there were some interesting experiences.

Apparently upon rebuild, the Danes renumbered parts not customarily numbered. Virtually all the Italian bolts bore rather large serial numbers, and few of the American ones did. One Italian bolt sported *two* numbers. The band and stock hardware of one rifle that I thought to be very early appeared to be covered with heavy rust; I sprayed the lot with Break-Free, let the assortment soak in the hot Arizona sun for days, and then boiled and boiled and boiled, sometimes with detergent. The effluent from this proved not to be rust at all, but some kind of seemingly evergreen-based preservative, which permanently stained everything it touched. Underneath was an almost perfect set of hardware, which appeared to be in a near-black finish, matching yet!

I also began to find beautiful, heavily flame-grained French walnut handguards, so stunningly colored that they looked odd with any stock I owned. These mainly bore "PB" bands and ferrules, and I am quite sure they were original to Italian rifles. I traded these off too early, then got a buttstock in the same stunning wood. I found only one cracked stock. There was only one birch buttstock.

My cache of Italian parts grew steadily, and I stumbled onto a Danish Beretta receiver and purchased it immediately, calling upon Derrick Martin to barrel it with almost indecent haste. This I tested with an Italian barrel initially, then set that .30-caliber unit aside and rebarreled with one of Springfield's units in .308/7.62 NATO and an original Beretta steel magazine block. (More about this later.)

Breda and More

The Danish-issue Breda I examined and have attempted to picture here is one of the very few that entered the United States before the ban took effect. It is it is basically the same as the Beretta Armi Roma Italia currently in my rifle rack. I've now had the opportunity to examine Italian rifle

An Italian trigger housing off a Breda M1. Note that the housing was Beretta, and everything else was coded "BMB" or "BMR" on this assembly.

receivers of the general M1 configuration from a rather large time frame, and I can draw some educated guesses. On all Italian M1 and BM59 receivers, examination with loupes and microscopes for tool marks, machining style and techniques, and the general manufacturing "fingerprints" strongly indicates that all were produced almost identically, inferring a common manufacturer, identical tooling, perhaps even common hands and eyes. I will not burn it in stone or write it in blood (remember, "NEVER SAY NEVER"), but it appears that the receivers were *all* produced in the same place or, at the very least, under the same management. However, peripheral parts bearing different makers' markings seem to be made with slightly to moderately different machinery and tools.

This suggests—but *does not* prove—that receivers came from a common source or were at least made with common supervision, but that subordinate parts and assemblies were, indeed, made at other locations. And it is virtually certain that rifles were shipped to the end user from separate locations/sources. There also seems to have been common Italian parts subcontracting, for collectors have noticed since the first Italian M1s were seen that "PB," "BMR," and "BMB" small parts are almost always mixed on rifles that seem to be original and undisturbed.

The lettering with which parts are marked seems to have gone through many almost random permutations as well. "PB," in particular, appears on bands, ferrules,

Very few World War II barrels were found among the Danish kits, but all proved to be in excellent condition.

A flame-grained French walnut handguard. Obviously made by Beretta, and the band/clip is so marked.

buttplates, gas cylinders, and gas cylinder lock screws in several sizes and type styles, and the other markings also show some variation in type style and size.

Also interesting: I've seen a number of Italian parts, marked with simply the part number, sometimes the *World War II* part number, and no other identifier of any kind. I've seen at least two gas cylinders that had to be late American wartime production, because of the other letters and hardness test marks, but

bearing "PB" aft of the stacking swivel. Indeed, the Winchester narrow wartime cylinder on the WIN-13 I photographed some years ago, a DCM gun, had been aftermarked "PB" at some time in its life. No one will ever explain all these anomalies, but the die-hard collector should remember that Beretta rebuilt M1s as early as the 1940s and apparently received some brand-new U.S.-produced parts along with their tooling. Again, it bears repeating that rifles are built to shoot, not to conform to collector's specifications.

Markings

The receivers found on the Danish rifles do not differ in configuration from other Garands, but the markings go a long way toward confirming what previously had been educated guesses. The Italian receivers built for Denmark all bear a crown and "FKF" shown in the photos on p. 28. FKF may somehow relate to Danish King Frederik IX, and the crown definitely denotes "by royal authority." But the most likely meaning of FKF is *Forsvarets Krigsmaterial Forvaltning*, meaning, (approximately) "Defense War Material Authority."

The author's "Beretta Armi Roma Italia," shown here after being converted to 7.62 NATO and used to test Springfield's new barrel in that caliber.

Breda's rendition of a Danish-issue M1. Examination with microscopes and instruments suggests common manufacture of all Italian receivers, though not of other parts.

The Breda barrels are marked with "BMB" and a variation of the part number, and "B.SID" and what appears to be a lot number or heat-treat batch, then a date. The one I shot said (topside, ahead of the chamber), "B.M.R. D35448," with the Italian cross proof, and on the right, where the operating rod slot would allow it to be viewed when in wood: "B.SID.71 1955" (1955 very obviously being the barrel date). Despite the World War II part number, flats and gas cylinder port are chrome-plated, meaning the tube meets the postwar new production and rebuild specifications. This particular barrel carried the Beretta code but was apparently originally produced for the Breda rifle. There was obviously some kind of interplay between the two manufacturers, even at this early date.

More precisely, my correspondence with

Beretta and articles in the Garand Collectors Association newsletter have confirmed that the B.SID denotes *"Breda Siderurgica,"* code for the Breda Iron and Steel conglomerate based in Brescia. "BMB," of course, is *"Breda Meccanica Bresciana,"* at that time a state-owned manufacturing facility directly related to "BMR," or *"Beretta Maschina (or Meccanica) Roma,"* the Rome-based firm that seems to have produced mainly smaller parts. Among my unusual treasures (and now on my Rome-marked Beretta) is a "BMR"-marked extractor, the only maker-identified extractor for the M1 I have yet seen, though I've seen some other strangely marked ones.

One .30 barrel among all the kits I looked at was merely marked "PB" with the postwar part number, no date, and a few small stamped inspector's marks and a cross proof. This, I suspect, might have been a Beretta replacement barrel.

All the barrels met the American specification in terms of grooves (four), contours, dimensions, and so on.

A COMBINATION OF NEW MERCHANDISE AND OLD ARTIFACTS FOR SHOOTING PLEASURE

The military M1 receivers of the past are now available as slightly overpriced parts from the CMP and whatever leftovers dealers have salted away from the "gravy days" of the M1 imports, or perhaps salvaged and torn down from rifles with tired barrels. In 1998 and early 1999, I was able to procure a couple myself and, as I prepared this book for publication, I was happy that I had because it turned out there was much to be done.

Receivers

The receivers I'd put away for future use and reference were a Springfield "reheat" 1.4 million, a 3.8 million late-war Springfield, a 3.3 million SA, and, of course, the aforementioned Beretta Roma. (More about those later.) But I also had lots of parts. And my *intention* for this tome was to put much of the other material I'd squirreled away on brand-new receivers, test it, and save the best for myself. The 3.8 million eventually wound up being tested here, along with my Beretta, with Springfield's new four-groove commercial barrel. But the idea was to test some other new tubes on brand new receivers. So much for good intentions.

Only Century has actually delivered any. The Entréprisé, advertised for quite some time, exists only in prototype form as this is written. The IAI, which has not been advertised but has been shown around the country, may actually reach the U.S. market before the Entréprisé. The Springfield Armory, Inc. receivers, which were covered in *The Complete M1 Garand*, went back on the market as "new items."

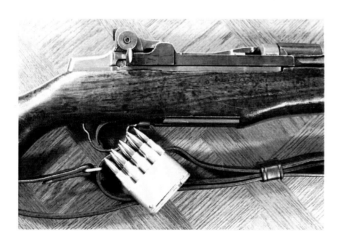

Regardless of caliber, all M1 clips are the very same unit. This one is loaded with .308 cartridges.

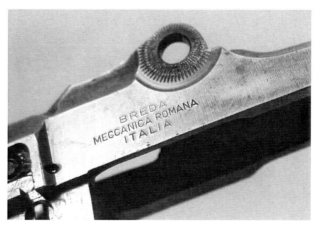

Left receiver panel data on a Danish-issue Breda-built M1 Garand.

Beretta M1 Garand markings stand for "Beretta Maschina Roma." Breda markings are almost identical, but the code is BMB.

My Century Arms gun featured a Danish barrel. I checked over the cast receiver very carefully. Markings are small, on the left side of the receiver, as seen on p. 32, and the finish is a nice phosphate. Adjacent parts have been refinished in a dark phosphate. I checked lockup and verified timing before shooting. The rifle was in .30/06, and so I dipped into my supply of Federal 3006GM and Century's PMP for a brief test shoot at "The Bowl" north of Mesa. This was necessary because the range was closed that day. It proved to be a very short test of function due to the presence of a number of shooters who had no grasp of safety procedures and our general discomfort with people drinking large quantities of beer while they actually shot firearms. The rifle cycled properly, seemed fairly accurate, and placed the valuable brass where we could find it before we left. I was somewhat miffed that the new receiver showed only the center alignment windage witness/reference marking, rather than the fine cuts on the old originals, but once we got the rifle rough sighted, this was less irritating than I had imagined.

About a week later, having cleaned the rifle, I took the same ammunition supply plus some Sierra molycoated 168-grain handloads using my optimized "Varget" load (the same one published in *The Complete M1 Garand*), 45.1 grains, with Federal's Match Large rifle primers. I am very stingy with .30/06 ammunition, since it costs so much more than .308. My friend Dave Lanza primarily executed the handloads, with input from Lee Templin. The bore had been meticulously cleaned of all copper fouling before shooting and then de-oiled and moly-prepped just before firing. The plan was to shoot about 350 rounds, then hand the rifle over to Lee Templin for further testing, upon which it was

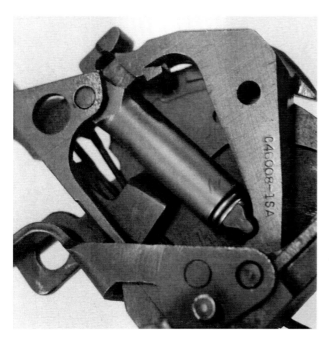

A very early hammer marked "C46008-1SA" with the extra hole, accompanied by many much later parts, found in one of the Century Danish kits.

Entréprisé Arms prototype receiver.

my intention to report further if any significant deviations developed. They haven't.

Even before the first test, in what has become almost a ritual, I went over the stock and used DUCO wood hardener and little bits of Crazy Glue (that's right, regular, ordinary Crazy Glue) in areas where stock fit seemed sloppy. This is not a real substitute for glass-bedding a rifle, but it is enough to stabilize a receiver temporarily for a short-term test without having to spend a lot of time or money. I particularly look for light passing under the receiver horseshoe, and, if necessary, build up that area, which in this case was necessary. In porous areas, I use the hardener and sometimes bits of filled epoxy before I even consider the rifle ready to be fired. I might not do this with a pure-as-the-driven-snow collector's rifle, but when I am testing barrels and/or receivers—and in this case, it was both—I do not want wood to be a factor at all.

Likewise—and this hasn't been necessary on anything built up from Danish parts kits—I will, at the first sign of wobble on a gas cylinder assembly, punch-peen the channels that receive the gas cylinder. Remember, any sideways wobble in the gas cylinder will destroy accuracy, even if everything else is perfect, and there's no point in shooting expensive ammunition without looking to these two small, easily-dealt-with potential problems.

Another check: are the rear sights secure? It has been a while, but a worn-out sight cover can cause even the very stable Type 3 rear sight assembly to move with recoil. I've also had cracked shafts and worn-out threads, though, again, none of this showed up with the Danish equipment. But it still must be checked. Wishing to test the rifle rather than myself (I am nowhere near as steady as I used to be and far more farsighted), I was determined to fire every round with the rifle carefully rested and bagged. This is asking for a sore shoulder, for confining recoil to a horizontal plane increases the rifle's thrust into the deltoid area.

Naturally, before shooting, I removed any and all thin oils from the M1 and properly greased the rifle with my favorite wheel bearing

31

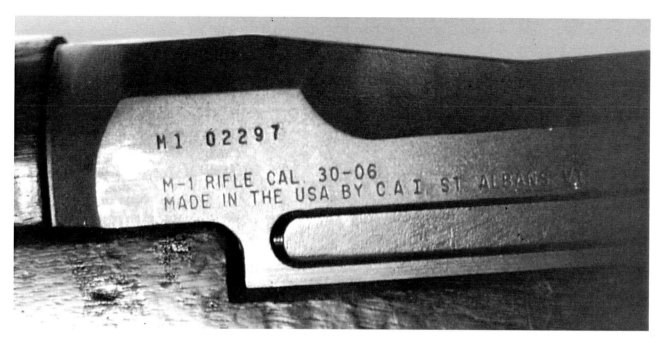

Logo of the author's early Century receiver. Nothing topside on the horseshoe at all. . . .

grease. I have not used what most people call "gun oil" on a firearm for almost 20 years. I do not consider it a lubricant. For the M1 Garand, and for any other fast-firing weapon, it will not stay where it is put and serves no meaningful purpose. I do sometimes use oil-based solvents for various purposes (mainly cleaning), and before storing guns I often use a high-grade motor-oil patina in bores and chambers, preferably Mobil 1 Synthetic. Naturally, to avoid case separations due to hydraulic adhesion, chambers must be cleaned of such lubricants before firing. I am convinced that wet and dirty chambers are also a factor in the "slamfires" mentioned later in this book. And bores should be "de-oiled" properly before molycoated bullets are fired. It was while I was preparing the Century receiver for its second test that an associate—who owned my first M1 book but apparently had never read it—confessed that he was having function problems with his M1. (Reason: IMPROPER LUBRICANTS. Oil leaves; grease doesn't.) So I greased it properly, took it to the range with me, and fired about 75 rounds of his handloads, never experiencing any of the problems he had described. I ran off a copy of the "troubleshooting" data in the book and

wrote on top of it: "Rifle fine. Lubrication sucks." I have moderated my views somewhat and now use white lithium grease on guns that will not see heavy use. But for purposes of fast-operating firearms, the rule is real simple: OIL IS NOT A LUBRICANT!

Even during World War II, the GIs who got the best service from their Garands were using concoctions of soft pencil lead and high-temperature cooking grease on the operating rod raceway. Nobody had to tell them that; they found out very quickly that *oil doesn't work!*

I wanted to shoot all the molycoated bullets first on the prepped bore, and, for the sake of those who don't handload, follow with the factory stuff. I shot my initial groups at 50 yards, since the earlier episode had not really confirmed that the sights were close to right, and the heat was sufficient that mirage might not reliably allow me to see bullet strikes at 100 yards with the spotting scope.

Having blasted mainly at the 300-yard gong with the rifle that "wasn't working"—and having had no malfunctions of any kind—I put out the little small-bore target I like to use at 50 yards and slowly tracked into the target bull. Eleven shots in, I was striking just above dead center of the little red stick-on center and cutting half-inch three-shot clusters.

Satisfied that I was sighted properly, I rotated my spotting scope over to some other targets at 100 yards and played with the power settings. I could discern the .50-caliber holes from someone's huge muzzle-loader, but another gentleman was shooting to my left with a .270-caliber heavy target rifle, and the mirage was such that I could not tell his bullet holes from tiny crinkles in the paper. In fact, unless that huge rifle was missing completely, my first impression was that I couldn't even discern his groups. Later, I realized that I could in fact find his five-shot clusters, which were excellent, but everything much smaller was "iffy" . . . so my decision was to try this rifle, that day, at 75 yards, which I proceeded to do, placing my targets during the next cease-fire.

At 75 yards, I got no group larger than 1.25 inches with the Sierra molycoated bullets, and we are discussing eight-shot groups here. Five would sometimes be under the traditional 1-inch standard, center to center. The 3006GM 168-grain loads shot almost identically.

Again, when testing ammunition and hardware, I clean between types of ammunition, including at least a moderate copper solvent cleanup, even if I have not been using metal-jacketed bullets. Call it superstition, but I refuse to test a product of any kind under anything save clean conditions, and I believe in fouling shots only within the short span of a magazine or so.

Pretoria Metal Pressings (PMP) ammo, imported from South Africa by Century, goes for around $9 to $10 a box in many stores, half or less the price of 3006M, so I didn't expect a great deal from it. Also, almost everyone I know who shoots the M1 has the distinct and documented impression that bullets of 155 grains up to about 180 grains usually shoot best, and the PMP fodder was loaded with a 143-grain Spitzer.

However, it shot very nicely—nothing over 1 1/2 inches, and several five-shot subgroups under an inch (and this with an untuned rifle and some wind). There were no flyers (unusual for me, since I generally generate a few on my own), and there were no failures to function. I resolved to touch up the trigger a bit before passing the rifle on to Lee Templin, and to look at the barrel and receiver to see if anything had happened (e.g., cracks, odd bits of metal). I did find some brass "dust" down in the magazine well, typical of a crisp, new, extractor, freshly finished, and made a note that if I shot it much more, I would smooth those mating surfaces very gently.

Upon later detailed cleaning of the gas system, I found powder residue to be no more and no less than one would expect from this level of firing. Examination of the brass showed nothing unusual. The main thing I learned was that the Danish surplus barrels, if in sound condition, can deliver accuracy within match specifications without being in a match-prepared rifle. Detailed disassembly revealed an unusually tight front handguard and actual contact between the stacking swivel lug of the gas cylinder and the handguard. Modifying these tiny fits, all by themselves, would probably have resulted in at least slightly better performance.

The rifles sell for $389 to $479 in stores. Of course, I cannot guarantee that your barrel will be as good as mine. What I can assure you is that the rifles are, in fact, assembled by someone with a solid knowledge of the Garand, and that some of the details not checked by others seem to be subjected to Century's inspection. This is important.

I am sure someone, somewhere will have some kind of negative experience with somebody's new receiver. This happened, we all forget, even with original GI rifles. And with Fed Ord material it was chronic.

These rifles—because of their civilian receivers—will never have the collector's value of GI M1s, but they are credible shooters. I have since eyeballed, handled, and even taken down to small parts a variety of M1s in inventory at area stores and in the hands of shooters, and I have yet to find any of the errors of casting and assembly that one expects to see sooner or later with a relatively embryonic product. So for the person who wants to shoot but flinches at the price of an all -GI M1 or a prepared match rifle, the Century-receivered rifles appear to serve as useful, handy alternatives.

Barrels of Barrels

I had only just finished an exhaustive test of Citadel's best grade match M1 barrel and Springfield's last generation match barrel when I found out Citadel was out of business, and the Springfield "upper level" stuff had changed considerably. Too bad. Both were pretty good products. And besides, I had spent a small fortune on ammo for testing products that no longer existed, at least not on the open market, though there is no telling how many of each may repose at the back of some smith's shop. I therefore acquired SA's new standard barrel, this one somewhat more like the GI unit than the old six-groove, and the Fulton Armory standard grade in both .308/7.62 and .30-06. As this is written, my master plan calls for the .30-06 FA barrel to be bolted to my last spare receiver as soon as I build up an ammo supply for the older cartridge. The SA I ordered only in .308, planted on my Beretta Roma rifle, and duly tested it, and the .308/7.62 Fulton barrel went right on my 1.4 million "reheat," whereupon testing began immediately.

"Immediately" is not entirely true. I use a very conservative polish technique on new barrels before even beginning to break them in. Some people call this "lapping," but I don't use lapping compound or other traditional supplies. I use automotive liquid polishing compound on patches, making literally thousands of passes; meticulously wiping out the dried residue with oversized patches until the bore is virtually mirror-like, always according to directions; then cleaning with solvent and synthetic motor oil and rubbing again; and finally degreasing thoroughly and preparing the bore with whatever molycoat preparant is at hand. This treatment, which is really just very fine polishing and should not change anything one can measure with normal instruments, eliminates some of the eccentricities of an M1 barrel's early life.

New barrels tend to copper-foul badly and shoot erratically for the first several hundred rounds of their shooting lives, and if there are eccentricities near the gas port on the M1 and similar rifles, this will tend to be exaggerated. Again, this happens with all rifles due to microscopic burrs, inclusions, and tool marks, which tend to be mitigated and disappear as the rifle is shot and can merely be highlighted by gas-operation systems with such anomalies near their ports. But there is a subordinate theory that such surface irregularities cause other irregularities, in turn harming both barrel life and accuracy. I refuse to fully endorse this theory, but on the other hand I will state it as a suggestion and tell you, affirmatively and for sure, that this little operation will provide the best part of an M1's accuracy much earlier and make a rifle under test much easier to clean. Therefore, even if all of the other asides and theories are wrong, I have a small hand-labor process that allows the saving of the stinkiest part of the work on the dirty end of shooting.

I should probably add, since I was unable to fully work up the FA .30-06 for test. Much of the reason was my fitting a Marlin postwar barrel from among the Danish kits to the other late war receiver, the 3.3 million, to do a little work that sprang from curiosity. I had fired some oddities, including a button-grooved tube that bore a Marlin commercial logo and oddments of military markings that may have gotten into military inventory via some enterprising, curious armorer decades before my purchase; an "SAC" of apparently approximately World War II vintage, which I was told was made by Savage; and an "MAC," with full World War II-style markings, lacking even the chrome flats and gas port. These I had purchased for very little money at Surplus Disposal at Fort McCoy in Wisconsin many years ago, and, according to some people, these *cannot* exist, let alone in military ownership. Same with the "SBC," which I saw and noted there, and bought, but sold before ever fitting it to a rifle. The "MAC" and the "SAC"—I have since located another "SAC" and photographed it—bore vintage military markings, and seemed

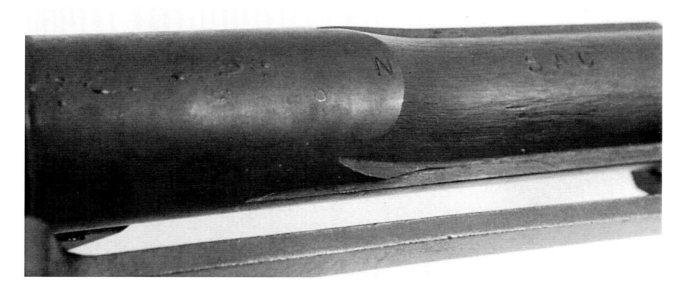

"SAC"-marked barrel of World War II style and configuration. The author has seen a couple of these. Also seen, bearing part number 35448 and mostly in government ownership at the time are "SBC," "RA," and "MAC." There is some doubt that Remington made M1 receivers under the "T" programs, but some collectors think Remington made barrels.

to be of World War II vintage. Along with the button-rifled Marlin, they shot very nicely with ball ammunition, but the button-rifled Marlin opened up with heavier bullets.

I also purchased and then resold what appeared to be a postwar barrel marked "RA," not dated, but with the World War II part number. At the time, I thought this sort of disposal would go on forever and never envisioned myself doing books like this. Thing is, the Marlin postwar tube found in one of the kits measured virtually new on the throat erosion gauge, and I wanted to try it with high-quality handloads. The tube was slightly disappointing, to quickly summarize this test, which was not done with this book in mind. It more than met service specifications, but with ammo at $1.50 per round, like 3006GM and the very best handloads, one expects to see at least one five-shot array with all rounds touching. Yet, despite my best efforts and allowing the best rifle shot I know to blast out eight rounds, 1 1/2 inches seemed to be the best result, and that with a great deal of preparation. Now, it is possible that this barrel, had I polished it like a truly new unit or broken it in gradually, might have approached the level of postwar commercials. But my experience is that military barrels—save

LMRs, some National Match units, very late H&Rs and, of course, the Danish unit just mentioned—seldom equal even low-priced current units. And why should they? There are almost 50 years of machining technology advances and measurement behind the newer units, not to mention anything that might have happened, even to a technically "new" unit, over all that time.

Shooters should gravitate toward newer barrels in either caliber for two very sound reasons: (1) vintage military barrels have high collector values if they are in solid condition and are irreplaceable, and (2) new commercial units will virtually always (a rule to which the exceptions are very notable) shoot much better.

Which brings me to a brief summary of the new barrels under review.

The Springfield Armory unit makes no attempt at mimicking military markings, though external dimensions forward of the handguard slots are absolutely correct.

The Springfield unit carries the maker's name and ".308" in the right operating rod cutout. Its gas port measured approximately 5/64 inch, correct for .30-06 but about 1/64 inch small for .308/7.62, which calls out .100 inch. A standard 3/32-inch drill bit is close enough, and I enlarged the port. Note, however, that if you are a long-range shooter who wishes to push large bullets supersonically at great range, you should talk to your smith before modifying the gas port. There seemed to be more metal, about .0016 inch, over the chamber area, and I could not fit a standard GI rear/upper hand guard to the unit. This did not matter, since I already had a hollowed-out unit on hand. These hollowed-out handguards—you can use a router; I use 60-grit sandpaper—will increase accuracy all on their own by reducing pressure on the barrel and improving airflow around it. With anything that I know will be shot much, the handguards are hogged out, though I seldom remove the front handguard tin liners anymore except on a true, pure match rifle. I have experimented with drilling many small holes in that unit and buffing until it is just short of transparent, but removing the liner means that the stock ferrule and bands and even the handguard itself can eventually shoot loose and begin to bounce around. This is irritating, ugly, and not good for accuracy. I am seeking, frankly, a better way to do all the front handguard work-ups, without a lot of endless misery, and when I find it, I will execute it on all my rifles.

The Fulton Armory barrels bore military markings (the .308, with the late number for 7.62 barrels, F11010457, was dated 9-98, and coded "FA"). Its gas port was properly sized, and external dimensions were right off the GI drawing.

The "match" Springfield .308, which now graces my friend Pat Fisher's 3.8 million rifle that used to be mine, was of almost identical configuration to the "standard" barrel, though the internal polish was of a higher order, and the gas cylinder fit was miserably tight.

The .30-caliber Fulton unit also employed military-style markings, only the correct postwar part number, D6535448, was in the operating rod slot and the date was 12-98.

Like most civilian barrels, the flat forward of the threads, usually called the shank or shoulder, needed to be turned down slightly before the

barrels could be fitted to receivers in good condition, this from about .008 inch on the Springfield to roughly twice that on the Fulton units (both of the Fultons will require the exact same amount of reduction). This is done because new barrels sometimes have to be put on old receivers, which may have been sandblasted or even belt-sanded, and whose external dimensions in areas like those surrounding the barrel threads may have been reduced to remove pitting. This is a sound approach and was done on many late GI replacement barrels for precisely the same reasons.

Both received my hand-polish treatment. It's worthy of note that the Fulton, depending on from whom purchased, usually sells from $30 to $50 higher than the standard Springfield, though for somewhat less than Springfield's match tube. Finish on both was very nice, the Fulton approaching the black of the wartime Winchesters, the Springfield a nice, uniform dark phosphate.

I fitted both rifles with Italian steel magazine blocks, so as not to accidentally try to jam a .30-caliber clip in either, since at this stage I thought I would be actively testing both calibers simultaneously. I used "NM" modified gas cylinders on both, along with the aforementioned relieved handguards, and tightened up the stocks via my customary "quick" method. Both guns received the smoothing operations described to ejector and extractor and my "foolproof" trigger job, as did Pat's 3.8 million rifle bearing the "match" Springfield barrel. Precleaning and prefiring lubrication procedures were followed as described earlier with the Century gun.

My ammo supply was vastly more liberal in .308/7.62. In addition to 168- and 155-grain Sierra molycoated match bullets loaded in selected brass ahead of Varget charges, I had a good stock of 168-grain 308GM from Federal and several cases of British "Radway Green" ammo originally loaded, I am told, for British Army Special Air Service (SAS) snipers. This stuff had been shooting beautifully in some more casual experiments, and I was eager to try

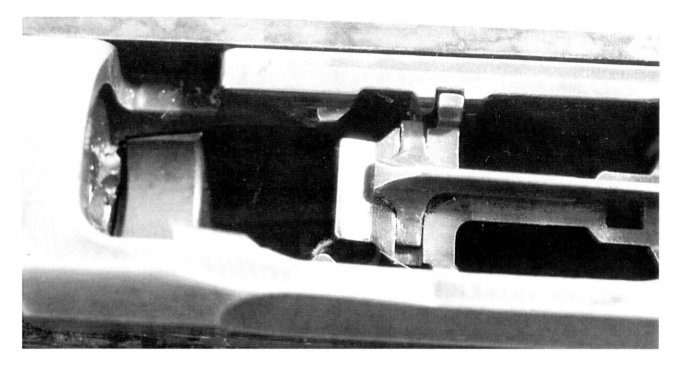

Italian steel magazine blocks may be fitted to any M1, to avoid the troublesome jams that eventuate trying to feed .30-06 ammo to a .308/7.62 rifle.

it in a part accurized and considerably smoothed Garand.

Each rifle was fired, rather casually, at the 300-yard gong before being even seriously sighted in, then bore-cleaned and prepped for molycoated bullets. The 155 Sierras very rapidly proved to be extremely accurate at 100 yards, both rifles putting eight rounds at least once under the 1-inch magic parameter. Later, the other ammunition would prove not to be far behind.

From the beginning, the Fulton proved to be slightly more accurate and, in fact, precisely equaled the performance achieved later with the match version of the Springfield barrel, although in rapid fire (which I got around to later), the very slightly heavier Springfield barrel shot identically—perhaps a matter of luck, or perhaps something to do with the harmonics of a heavier barrel, albeit very slightly so, in rapid fire.

Before I became exhausted (which isn't very long at 110° Fahrenheit), I began to do some fairly interesting plinking at the 300-yard gong. The Fulton delivered at least one five-shot cluster small enough that I could not discern, with the mirage at 100 yards, whether I had missed. Center to center, it was 5/8 inch . . . . Oddly, it was with the British ammunition, not the far more expensive commercial stuff or the expensive handloads. The "Radway Green" did not seem to hold this accuracy out at 300 yards quite as well as the other loads. But then, one doesn't expect lighter bullets to retain their accuracy quite as far out, though the difference here was *very* small. It was still very good ammo for the price.

I made a point of shooting both rifles several more times before coming to any firm conclusions. The Fulton "standard"-grade barrel, at least mine, performed fully to match specifications and beyond consistently—again, on a rifle not fully match prepared. This is impressive performance. The Springfield was not far behind and, indeed, in my hands and those of other shooters would periodically shoot as well and even, very occasionally, a tiny bit better. Both represent a high order of quality and dollar value.

Both firms offer an extensive list of services for the M1 as well. All my installation work on these rifles was done by Derrick Martin, one of

Stainless Krieger in 7.62/.308.

the few smiths who has yet to mount one of my barrels askew.

I will continue my research with barrels and ammunition for as long as I can get the work done. Again, I have to emphasize this point: neither of these barrels is the equal of the big Krieger, but most shooters will seldom notice the difference. And, of course, most of that difference will come when the barrel is hottest. And these barrels cost less than half the price of a Krieger.

We'll discuss some other concepts and toys later in this book; but, again, for the shooter of the M1 the world certainly has not ended.

CHAPTER 4
M1 GARAND'S MULTIPLE "FLAWS": A REALISTIC VIEW OF PERCEIVED PROBLEMS

Not all of the negative press the M1 received in its early days was false. The rifle did cost three or more times the price of the '03 Springfield, and its introduction was accompanied by some unreliability and a great deal of exaggeration thereof. But all of this has to be put in some kind of historical and factual perspective.

Garand's early designs were for a brand-new 7mm cartridge. But by about 1932, because of huge inventories on hand and the prevailing Depression economy, it was decided that the new rifle would have to use .30-06 ammunition, much of it dating from 1918 or earlier.

GAS TRAP IS A POWDER TRAP

None of the "gas trap" rifles ever built—in the United States, Germany, Russia, Belgium, or Britain—stayed in issue very long; most, in fact, were never issued at all. And they had problems in common.

In the Garand, the gas trap is more straightforward than most. The barrel ends some 2 inches behind a false muzzle, leaving a profound tube-shaped 2-inch reaction area for hot gasses. This very volume of gas, with slower burning powders—as my smith Jake explained in his shorthand—was what caused Jake, and the other half-dozen or so veteran armorers and team captains with whom I discussed the early M1 rifle, such profound problems in the field and in competition in the period 1936–40 that it constituted a crisis. Burning powder, ash, residues, and even bullet fragments accumulated in that relatively vast chamber, and what Jake called "secondary ignition"—just like dieseling in your gas-engined car—caused erratic performance, erosion at the muzzle, and build-up of complex fouling, such that the entire assembly really should have been removed for detailed cleaning after every few clips. The slower the powders, the more profound this symptom.

There seems to be no confirmation of this information among official documents at Aberdeen or Springfield Armory, but every smith of 1930s to early 1940s vintage who was involved with the rifle in its early days used almost the same words. The speed with which the gas trap's more traditional replacement, the old "gas port" system (used on machine guns since the 1890s), was instrumented and standardized suggests that the negative results of the reversion to the old .30-06 chambering were well known in the field. By 1938, experimental gas port rifles were already under test, and not long after the middle of 1940, no more gas trap rifles were scheduled for production.

Similarly, the German G41, in both its Walther and Mauser incarnations, used a somewhat more subtle gas trap, employing barrel sleeves and even larger blast chambers early on, but the system worked on the same "foolproof" principle, and the machinery did all the same things. (With almost identical results, I hasten to add!) Their rifle—also intended to replace their bolt-action piece universally—saw some production and some issue, but once it was in the field, the same problems developed and it was preempted by another gas port semiautomatic, the G43/K43 series.

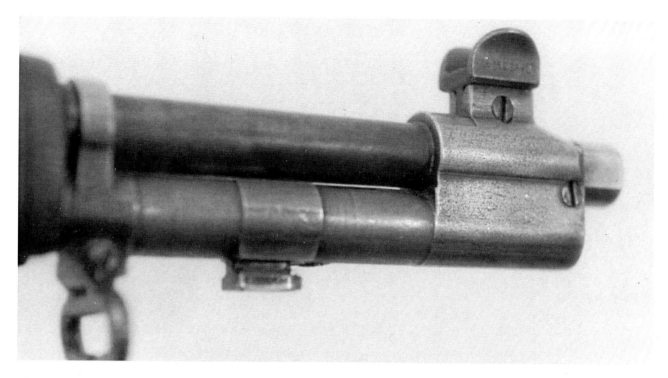

The gas trap never did work out in .30-06, though it might have worked fine with the experimental, interim .276 cartridge, using faster powders. The very latest of the gas trap cylinders cranked the outside "ears" aside slightly, but the more laborious takedown required remained.

From the onset, the gas port system worked better and required less attention than the gas trap system, which, once in production, was dumped for the more traditional type in use on machine guns since the 1890s. The upper one here is an early war unit, the lower one an International Harvester.

Jake was quick to point out that any kind of secondary ignition, especially when it is close to the muzzle, let alone right *at* the muzzle, in the immediate area of the bullet, causes terrible accuracy problems, beginning with bullet distortion and ending, downrange, with terrible vertical stringing. This can also be a safety problem. One veteran told me that early M1s often smoked heavily from their false muzzles, especially when fired with match ammo, long after they were returned to their range racks.

But like most of what is or was wrong with the M1, the gas trap system was a flaw because of outside factors. For instance, had the 7mm round for which the 1929–32 rifle was designed persisted and become standard, the gas trap probably never would have become an issue, let alone a problem. One of my many correspondents has fired his gas trap rifle with my handloads using BL(C)-2 powder and 168-grain bullets and reports no difficulties whatsoever in several hundred rounds of firing. But he notes that with issue ammunition (and this is a direct quotation), "The gas cylinder stinks and smokes and is a misery to clean, and it *must* be cleaned!"

This has nothing to do with corrosive ammunition, although when one views a cross-section of the gas trap, there is a *strong* possibility that the muzzle and adjacent areas would require detailed solvent and water cleaning to obviate wholesale rusting and pitting. Rifle powders before about 1936 were virtually all of current 4350 speed or slower, and the closer one gets to World War I stocks, the more common that speed range becomes. With a 22-inch barrel, burning and unburned particles of extruded powder—some as large as a retractable pencil lead in diameter—can actually cause physical interference, not to mention ballistic problems. Even a quick read through Speer's latest *Reloading Manual* (especially the powder illustrations) will give some idea of the potential effluents.

It is not at all amazing that virtually no footprints of causation remain at the official level. I keep hearing that there were only ever a handful—perhaps from two to five—T26 18-inch-barreled M1s in issue or under test, and that the related M1E5 "folding stock" project was similarly tiny. And yet for 36 years now, I've talked to men who claim they were variously exposed to such rifles. More interesting, I saw both new-condition 18-inch barrels and a collection of rather beat-up folding stocks for the Garand at Fort McCoy (then Camp McCoy) as early as 1964. I inquired about surplus disposition, speaking to a gentleman whose name, coincidentally, was Jim Thompson, and he looked at the specimens and tags. There were lots of them, in a huge pile, being sold at scrap prices. "All I can tell you," he replied, "is that they come from a couple of navy bases and from Fort Bragg." At a dollar or so apiece, I probably should have picked up some specimens, but I was looking for other, more practical toys at the time.

The bland statement that "the replacement of the gas trap cylinder seems to have been for other than functional reasons" has long been an easy write-off of what seems to have been something of an emergency. I have tested the theory, as have others, and the "slow powder/secondary ignition" physics are ironclad. However, it is the artifacts that prove the point: there are way too many guns numbered below 52000—that is, built until about September 1940—whose barrels and gas cylinders seem to have been replaced within one calendar year to validate a theory that replacement of gas trap mechanisms was anything but a very serious emergency. Winchester—and its very first "school" rifle appears in detail in *The Complete M1 Garand*—was never even given the gas trap drawings.

The entire front sight of the earliest series of rifles comprises straight verticals, including the shading "ears," meaning there was a strong possibility of mistaking one of the outside flats for the sight proper. The "furniture" on the gas trap cylinder was modified at different times and the sight slightly altered, but by 1939 all indications from the hardware suggest that engineers were aware that there was no point in attempting to improve the system.

Still, when the rifle was on John Garand's drawing board, the .30-caliber cartridge was not a factor, and it is likely that the earlier cylinder would have worked with a higher pressure curve (that is, more efficiently, with faster burning powders) cartridge. The Japanese—who are known to have had specimens of both types of rifle under test by early 1942 and who were trying to generate a semiautomatic rifle, though apparently not as a very high priority— seemingly had problems with their gas traps, too. Their surviving prototype rifles spun off the Garand use the gas port exclusively. Apparently, they had reached the same conclusion independently of the armorers and competitors in the field in the United States.

Most of us will never have to worry about keeping a gas trap operating, anyway. They are extremely rare and probably too valuable to shoot.

THE M1 IS TOO HEAVY

I am probably the last person in the world to accept that the M1 is "too heavy," since I put a lot of effort into trying to *increase* the weight and to modify the weight distribution of match/competition M1s. Almost any M1 weighs at least 10 pounds without the heavy leather sling, and a good many hover around 12 pounds (and more loaded with sling and bayonet). The "book" weight, from *Small Arms of the World*, is 9.5 pounds.

It was the Garand's weight and the excellent gas system that made the M1 the easy-shooting machine it was by soaking up recoil and generally stabilizing the rifle.

Here's a weight comparison of the Garand and some of its contemporaries (these are all empty weights).

RIFLE	WEIGHT (LBS.)
German G41(W)	11.08
German G41(M)	11.25
German G43	9.50
German MP44/STG44-45	11.50*
German K98k	8.60
U.S. Thompson M1928A1	10.75
U.S. Johnson M1941	9.50
U.S. Browning Automatic Rifle M1918A2	18.50
U.S. M1917 Enfield	8.18
U.S. Model 1903 "Springfield"	8.69
Soviet Tokarev M1940	9.48
Soviet Mosin-Nagant M91/30	8.70
Soviet SKS	8.80
Soviet PPSh 1941	8.90
Italian M41 rifle	8.21
Japanese Type 38	9.25
Japanese Type 99 (short)	8.60
British SMLE No. 1 Mk 3	8.62
British No. 4 Mk 1 rifle	8.80
U.S. M1 carbine	5.50
U.S. M1A1 carbine	6.19
Belgian SAFN Model 49	9.48
Typical FN FAL	9.06**

* These vary in weight even more than the M1.

** Due to variations in furniture, barrel weight, and so on, this represents the low end of FAL weights.

M1"too heavy"? That's a matter of taste. This match rifle, in extra-fancy flame-grained walnut, weighs almost 14 pounds, and the author would like to add a little "nose weight."

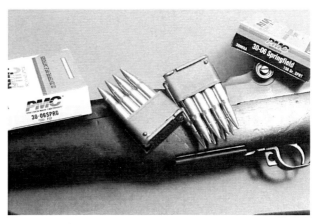

John Garand was stuck with an internal magazine, but it became the subject of much research by mid-World War II. The closed bottom of the M1 contributes to its integrity against dirt.

These weights are all from various editions of *Small Arms of the World* and my stock of military manuals. But what this comparison shows is that everything of power similar to the M1 that can be shot comfortably (and that omits the British No. 5 Jungle Carbine and the German G33/40 from that group, I think) is within about a pound of the Garand. Nearly everything semiautomatic or selective fire, regardless of power range, is about the same weight or heavier. Not only could a carbine-weight .30-06 or .308 be built, but it's been done; however, shooting such a lightweight repeatedly is a brutal thing, and such bits of fluff should be reserved for hunting.

I cannot and will not give somebody a pat answer that M1 is or is not too heavy—or, for that matter, too light. That's all about taste and physical endurance. Bear in mind that everything that went wrong with the spin-off of the Garand, the M14, happened because of overzealous efforts to lighten it without refiguring some very simple physics. M14s, in their original service form, weigh 8.7 pounds, but eventually, those intended for support automatic fire, such as the M14A1 and some sniper versions, gained well over four pounds— and often a bipod. The M16 is surely lighter than the M1 but, at 500 to 1,000 meters, is nowhere

near as deadly. Much of this doesn't matter in modern warfare, and it surely doesn't matter to a casual plinker. But the M1 was not intended for plinking, though it's very, *very* good at it.

MAGAZINE CAPACITY

Having saddled John Garand with an internal magazine requirement, ordnance authorities very rapidly began to experiment with insertable box magazines of increased capacity. Fine. This culminated in the M1E, the BM.59, and, for that matter, the M14. But Garand was stuck with the requirement.

Japanese prototypes almost immediately jumped to a 10-round box that could be topped off from strippers. However, this brings up the interesting question of the introduction of dirt into the mechanism from the bottom, which on the original M1 was virtually impossible unless the firing/trigger mechanism was removed. Most bolt rifles of the time, the British rifles excepted, carried six or fewer rounds but could be refilled before the magazine was empty.

For the times, however, eight rounds was plenty, and the general integrity of the action— that is, its "dirt exclusion"—was superb. But it sure would have been nice to be able to replenish the magazine from the top.

THE HANDGUARD SYSTEM

Because of the way they are used military rifles require handguards. Even with them, hand and forearm burns are common after heavy firing, and semiautomatics with big, long operating rods like the Garand's would catch on a lot of things and throw a lot of dirt without handguards. The M1, however, almost always shoots better with no handguards on at all. This was suspected for a long time but was finally proven by a series of detailed experiments that led to the National Match specifications and adjustments detailed in *The Complete M1 Garand*. The wood and metal fittings not only contribute to heat buildup along the barrel but expand and twist and generally put stress on the barrel and adjacent parts. Still, to delete the handguards in a service situation would cause far more problems than it would solve.

The "lower"—really, the rear upper—handguard (the one immediately forward of the M1 receiver) is a particularly nasty beast, along with its "band," actually a spring-steel retaining clip. It retains just fine if you can get it on a new handguard at all, and if you can then get it onto the barrel. I have used various fishing line openers and modified circlip pliers on them over the years and even briefly owned the military "wrench," but none of these is foolproof.

Hogging out both handguards will immediately contribute to accuracy, because the less contact there is between these and the barrel and receiver, the less obvious the torque/heat effects on the barrel and attendant assemblies.

Experiments were done from the early 1940s on to produce an "all-in-one" handguard set—sometimes of painted aluminum and sometimes of dyed-in-the-mass plastics—wherein the handguards and middle band were a single formed unit. Some of these even deleted the band/clip entirely. And they worked, but the plastics of the time tended to distort and cook, and the aluminum had to be refinished frequently and had the additional disadvantage of transmitting heat to the surfaces very quickly.

For the technology of the times, however, wood worked best, was available, and protected both the user's hands and body and the rifle's metal, so that we still have a great many rifles. So the "handguard flaw" involves a certain amount of misery for those of us who work on the rifles and clean them diligently, and a modern, high-heat version of the experimental one-piece set might be superior—if someone would produce such a beast in a manner that did not significantly alter the "look" of the rifle.

AH, SWEET MYSTERY OF TRAINING

Morons can operate the M1 only at considerable risk. And they can never seem to get it apart. This is just one of the many reasons the M1 has no real history of use by criminal gangs. The hand-eye coordination and sense of feel required to insert an eight-round clip without leaving some skin and blood inside the rifle's guts are, I'm sure, quite beyond the capabilities of any of the gangbangers in my neighborhood. Not too long ago, these lowlifes had a sort of gunfight with at least five long guns and a dozen pistols, in which the only shots fired came from a little .25 automatic and an old revolver. Nobody was being easy on anybody, and nobody hit anybody, either. They just couldn't properly load most of the hardware, and one dimwit in particular seemed unaware that he had to cycle the bolt on his SKS to get the first round where it had to be.

For someone who has no discipline or cannot read or follow instructions, the M1 is perhaps the worst rifle in the world. And for that, I am *very glad*. I've had only one incident in which an M1 caught a digit with its bolt, that about 10 years ago, when I was cleaning a particularly sweet match rifle. I got a phone call that required me to pass on quite a lot of information, and, of course, I should have set the rifle aside as soon as the phone rang. But I didn't. Having completed the bore cleaning and while chatting merrily away, I used a finger as a reflector off my high-intensity light to check my work. It must have struck the follower precisely correctly to release the bolt and operating rod, because my next sensation was a great deal of pain, and the weird sensation that my right index finger was growing even as it bled.

I not only had to open the rifle and clean it up but also to dress the wound and, while not really in the mood, make sure the blood didn't do more damage than sloppy cleaning could ever do. The man on the other end heard the noise and my expression of pain. It wasn't a phone call I could postpone, and I couldn't let the rifle or my finger just sit. And I kept rolling over repeatedly in my head that old admonition, "Never forget your training!"

My finger acquired the shape of a .30/06 round, albeit puffed up, and to this day has a small "bottleneck" from being effectively "chambered.". . . I can thus claim that I have never had "M1 thumb," but I have a permanent "M1 finger."

Stripping the M1, especially the bolt, operating rod, and trigger group/firing mechanism, requires training and repetition and considerable care. Also necessary are some mechanical intuition and a sense of feel that's adequate to know when something is not right. I once upon a time stupidly presumed this could be taught to anyone; it can't.

Perhaps the greatest "weakness" of the M1 Garand is that it requires some training, knowledge, discipline, and instinct to use, let alone maintain. I consider that, by the way, one of the rifle's greatest strengths, for it is an apparatus virtually useless to those who are unsuitable to own anything more dangerous than a spoon.

CHAPTER 5
THE M1'S DELIVERY CHRONOLOGY: WORLD WAR II AND POSTWAR

You may recall my carefully avoiding a date chart for M1 Garands in my earlier book. The reason is that such charts are, in a way, a trap: someone restoring a rifle may presume that they are somehow ironclad, perfectly accurate, and therefore a sort of religious law, never even to be challenged. So the first thing you need to know about this date chart (adapted from Duff's material—which is as close as you get to complete and accurate—and various other sources, plus a lot of my own notes since 1964) is this: *when a receiver was built or contracted for is merely a small part of the rifle's history!*

By no means do receiver "dates" correlate precisely to barrel dates, nor should they.

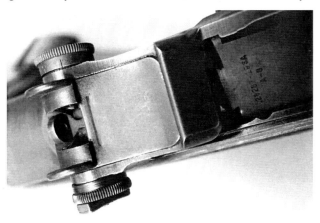

Collectors should do some analysis before presuming anything is wrong. This World War II rifle, numbered over 3 million, carried a sight cover much earlier. But the rifle seems never to have been rebuilt, and the finish matches perfectly. This doesn't mean it's original, just that this slightly reconfigured part has been on the rifle a long time and may be correct, even though much earlier than the rifle.

Barrel production was frequently 30 to 60 days ahead of or behind the production of other parts, especially receivers. And if a rifle was rejected or required adjustment for some reason, it could wind up leaving the factory with a barrel considerably later than its theoretical receiver date. Receiver dates and production groupings are, therefore, just one small part of the story.

Even though other collectors have told me similar stories, I am not any happier to have spent a long time looking for the "right" barrel for a particular rifle, only to find, either in the literature or by experience, that, in fact, the tube with which it arrived was the correct unit. You feel particularly stupid if you've gone to the trouble and expense to find the "correct" barrel and mount it and you no longer own the one that was truly right.

There are other factors: I recently received a letter from a man who was deeply concerned that his rifle with an approximately 100000 receiver serial number had none of the correct parts on it, and in fact stock, barrel, and so on were all ca. late 1944 to early 1945. Not only did I tell him not to worry, I also told him to appreciate the likelihood that he had a World War II combat veteran. Again, there's no way of absolutely proving that, but the general practice during World War II rebuilds was to waste as little as possible, and virtually everything on this rifle had apparently required replacement. Some accidents could cause such a condition, but combat damage is a very strong possibility.

Just as a slightly later barrel should not be of much concern, so small parts a month to a year earlier than the supposed receiver date shouldn't cause a collector to panic. Usable parts were never thrown out, and unless some flaw existed in a design, extant materials were used up as located. Even though this date chart is here under some protest (from me!), a good friend pointed out that a rifle's delivery date contributes to its legacy. And there's a purity to this that anyone can appreciate. I have therefore attempted to include enough notes and exceptions to make this material helpful.

World War II M1 production was nicely documented, and it is the very precision of these contract/delivery dates that sets the "trap" that sometimes confuses collectors. So as good as the data are, their key limitation is inherent: IT'S ONLY A DELIVERY DATE! Really, it's a *contracted* delivery date. A part

here and a part there do not make a rifle "incorrect." In some 36 years of fooling around with Mr. Garand's rifle, I've noticed with some regularity very late World War II rifles in nice, apparently original condition, bearing 1946 barrels, some with postwar "D35382" operating rods and "Type 3" sights. There is absolutely no way to prove it, but, at the very least, there is a strong possibility that these rifles were not fully assembled until many months after the war.

In the period 1932–36, 80 toolroom prototype rifles were produced, numbered to 80, and it may therefore be considered that "production"—slow at the onset—actually began in August 1937. This chart uses the numerical month abbreviation and the *last production number* for that month, thus using the "shorthand" similar to that actually used on the barrels. However, barrel dating was not present on many rifles before 1940, sometimes into 1941.

SPRINGFIELD 1937–1945

DATE	SERIAL #	DATE	SERIAL #
8-37	120	9-37	307
10-37	539	11-37	696
12-37	1034	1-38	1186
2-38	1338	3-38	1809
4-38	2213	5-38	2406
6-38/7-38	2911	8-38	3537
9-38	4386	10-38	5242
11-38	6072	12-38	6972
1-39	7715	2-39	8762
3-39	9893	4-39	10703
5-39	11511		

NOTE: At this time, reports from the field began to show up suggesting great difficulty in getting reliable performance from gas trap mechanisms, and various prototype gas port guns began to reach the field. Often, guns from mid-1939 to about September 1940 seem to have been "rebuilt," before ever leaving Springfield Armory, to the more reliable gas port configuration.

DATE	SERIAL #	DATE	SERIAL #
6-39	12848	7-39	12911
8-39	14823	9-39	17010
10-39	19410	11-39	21293
12-39	23567	1-40	26729
2-40	30008	3-40	33790
4-40	38034	5-40	41679
6-40	46221	7-40	51970

SPRINGFIELD 1937–1945

DATE	SERIAL #	DATE	SERIAL #
8-40	.59868	9-40	. 68054
10-40	. 78306	11-40	.90177

NOTE: Winchester contract kicked in December 1940. Winchester assigned "missing" serial numbers (Springfield had produced rifles numbered to 100000, then jumped to 165501), including instructional rifles beginning with "first" Winchester shown in *The Complete M1 Garand*. Springfield production for the month ended at serial number 169073.

DATE	SERIAL #	DATE	SERIAL #
1-41	.183519	2-41	.197811
3-41	.211228	4-41	.228527
5-41	.248757	6-41	.269686
7-41	.296252	8-41	.324301
9-41	.349442	10-41	.377258
11-41	.401529	12-41	.429811
1-42	.462737	2-42	.498216
3-42	.542494	4-42	.588879
5-42	.638679	6-42	. 691401
7-42	.749779	8-42	.809016
9-42	.872343	10-42	.940250
11-42	1008899	12-42	1090310
1-43	1169091		

NOTE: The second Winchester contract kicked in February 1943, so one "end" number is 1200000; lot numbers resume at 1357474 and continue to the last February issue, 1396225.

DATE	SERIAL #	DATE	SERIAL #
3-43	1469177	4-43	1547452
5-43	1629565	6-43	1710012
7-43	1786469	8-43	1877654
9-43	1978407	10-43	2092825
11-43	2204430		

NOTE: In December 1943 there was another Winchester contract crossover, wherein numbers ended (first lot) at 2305849, resumed at 2410000, and finished at 2420191 at the end of the month.

DATE	SERIAL #	DATE	SERIAL #
1-44	.2543412	2-44	2634316
3-44	.2723004	4-44	.2810628
5-44	.2900312	6-44	2981126
7-44	.3051952	8-44	3114434
9-44	.3180532	10-44	.3242497
11-44	.3302641	12-44	.3359159
1-45	3450503	2-45	.3531489
3-45	.3672442	4-45	.3717867
5-45	.3797768	6-45	3875601

NOTE: Various records draw various conclusions in this late period after June of 1945.

Receiver 97308, with early "flush nut" sights.

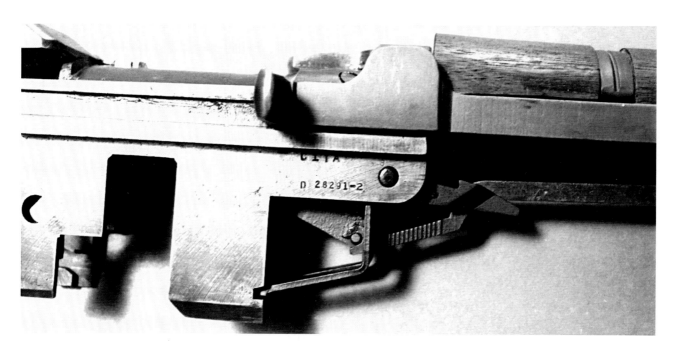

Very early Springfield receivers and most of the rest of the rifle closely resemble Winchester's output.

Small differences evolved in gas port Springfields from late 1940 (top) to 1942 (middle) and early 1943 (bottom).

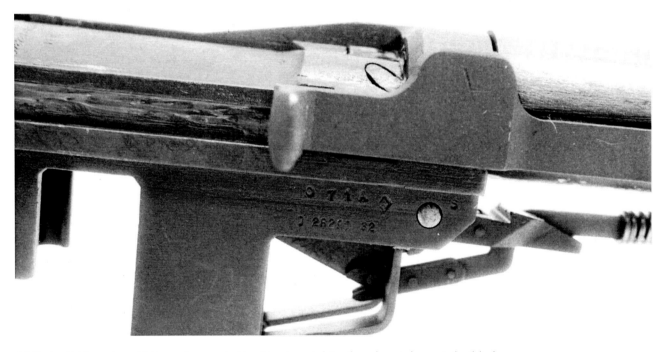

All Springfield-produced M1 receivers noted heat treatment data, though not always in legible form.

Receiver #208518.

SA receiver #481614.

The mill marks on this -17 M1 receiver, from about 1942, bespeak a worn out blade and are unusual for that late in M1 production at Springfield.

Receiver #462975, in a rebuilt condition, mounted in a laminated Boyd's stock.

Two midwar Springfield M1 receivers in the 2.5 million range.

In mid-1945, production slowed down in terms of complete rifles, and the last World War II number is considered to have been in the 3888000 range. Many of these are found with barrels dated just a few months later than that date, suggesting that they were not completed until well after the war. Also, at the very end, many experiments and new M1 developments at Remington and elsewhere caused a kind of confusion similar to "last casualty" malaise in the field, wherein the formerly meticulous record-keeping disappears, though guns were being delivered new to European-based units as late as 1947.

WINCHESTER 1940 TO LATE 1945

Winchester was a business first and foremost, and, as such, its prime goal was profit. Since Winchester barrels were not customarily dated, instead carrying the part number and a version of standard commercial proofs, the receiver dates are not quite as vital to putting together a restoration.

In addition, Winchester and Springfield sometimes slightly overlapped each other's production allocations. Approximately 30,000 Winchesters were produced in the range 357474 to well over 1387XXX (precise number unknown) in August/September 1943, and quite a bunch in the 2540000 range. These "duplicates" were frequently stamped with an "A" or etched below the number. The WIN-13 series receivers are primarily in the 1.6 million serial number range and comprise some very strange sets of parts, including some operating rods that are unmarked.

Winchester production began with 100,101 (shown in detail in *The Complete M1 Garand*), part of the "school" or "instructional" lot. Virtually all Winchesters were finished inky black, save for the WIN-13 series, which bore a

A comparison of a Springfield receiver from 1945 to a Winchester of similar vintage. Note, however, that many original Springfield receivers of the period 1942 and before were virtually as dark as the Winchesters.

DATE	SERIAL #	DATE	SERIAL #
12-40 to 1-41 "school lot" numbers 100101 to 100501			
2-41	100831	3-41	102701
4-41	104901	5-41	107801
6-41	111501	7-41	115501
8-41	20111	9-41	122081
10-41	126130	11-41	131130
12-41	137960	1-42	144110
2-42	149130	3-42	155310
4-42	162190		

NOTE: May 1942 was a contract "jump" point where the initial finished unit should have been 165500, then resuming at 1200001, finishing with 1203692.

DATE	SERIAL #	DATE	SERIAL #
6-42	1210472	7-42	1218972
8-42	1228982	9-42	1241002
10-42	1254002	11-42	1266502
12-42	1276102	1-43	1282762
2-43	1294762	3-43	1309772
4-43	1323872	5-43	1336882
6-43	1349982	7-43	1364982

NOTE: August 1943 was another contract "jump" point, where the initial lot finish was at 1380000, resuming at 2305850, finishing the calendar month at 2305932.

DATE	SERIAL #	DATE	SERIAL #
9-43	2318032	10-43	2334032
11-43	2523942	12-43	2533642
1-44	2379642	2-44	2394642
3-44	2409642	4-44	2424642
5-44	2439642	6-44	2454642
7-44	2469642	8-44	2484642
9-44	2499642	10-44	2513822
11-44	2523142	12-44	2533142

NOTE: January 1945 to the end of February 1945 was another contract "jump" point, this time constituting 2540XXX numbers, and groupings ending with 1601150 to 1605600 and, apparently, also 1607100, getting the WIN-13s out the door over the next few months. largely after the war. The WIN-13s were never really contracted for but were part of Winchester's insistence upon using up remaining parts, forgings, etc.

DATE	SERIAL #	DATE	SERIAL #
3-45	1613000	4-45	1620000
5-45	1627000		

The very first Winchester off the "school contract," 100001, with its data legend on the "horseshoe" burnished to show markings.

Gas cylinder detail on the very first Winchester M1.

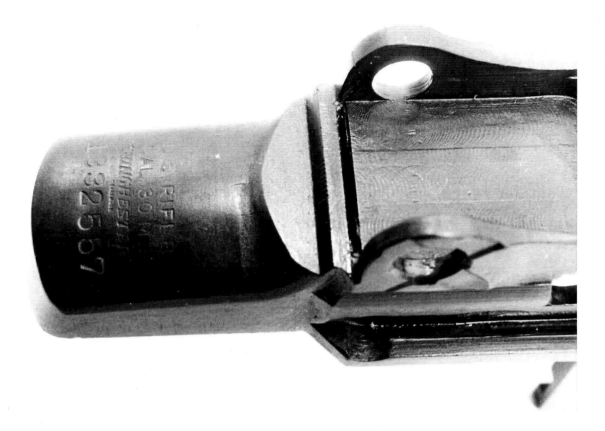

Winchester receiver #1332557.

Close-up of the muzzle end of a ca. 1944 Winchester. Note the single-slot gas cylinder lock screw and the wide "bent" sight "ears."

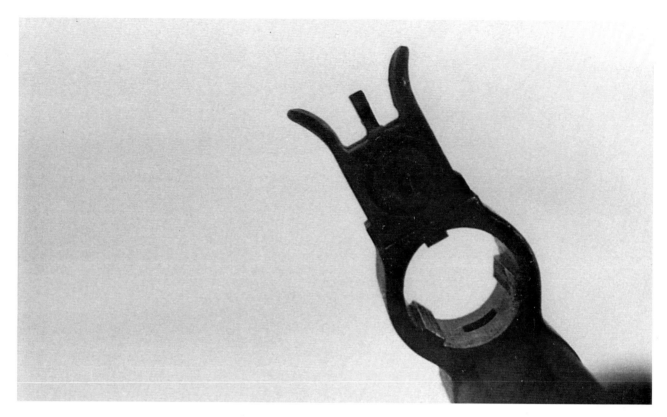

Rear detail of a Winchester M1 sight, off a WIN-13, mounted on the only wide-base gas cylinder the author has seen that might be by Winchester.

Winchester's WIN-13 receivers overlapped SA numbers and incorporated some of the changes from SA production of three to five years earlier.

A great many Springfield rifles like this one sport barrels and operating rods of Winchester production, and may have been part of some kind of parts interchange testing, actually released in issue. The author has also seen several of the reverse— Winchesters bearing Springfield barrels and operating rods of exactly the same date as when the Winchester receiver was supposedly delivered.

variety of colors and surfaces and finally began to catch up with some of the changes instituted at the armory during the war.

Winchester never built a gas trap rifle. That system had been discarded by December 1940. But most of the detail parts were of early pattern, and many stayed that way to the very end.

The very last Winchester bore an unknown serial number somewhere over 1640000 and was completed in June 1945.

A further Winchester anomaly of some interest to collectors: In *The Complete M1 Garand* I noted having seen several Springfield M1s bearing Winchester barrels and operating rods of precisely the same vintage and detail, suggesting that the long-held suspicion that parts-interchange programs were conducted at both manufacturing facilities was much more than a rumor. Since 1992, I have seen several more. Somewhat unnerving—and easier to

speculate about because of the attendant upgrades—is the fact that I have seen several Winchester rifles, apparently undisturbed, bearing dated Springfield barrels and operating rods correct for precisely that vintage. This prima facie evidence suggests— but does not absolutely prove—that these interchange test rifles were released into general issue.

POST-WORLD WAR II DATE INFORMATION: EXCEPTIONS AND NOTES

From 1945 to 1952, most production activity on the M1 dealt with prototypes, some by Remington, apparently newly built; others converted as convenient from earlier receivers; and a very tiny amount of production evidently almost hand manufactured, some of

From front to rear, representatives of all three U.S. postwar Garand manufacturers (International Harvester, Springfield Armory, and H&R), all from about 1955–56.

it apparently intended to edify machinists and personnel at new contractors. Considerable effort was directed toward getting Beretta's Garand program moving. International Harvester was prepared to get into the program with perhaps more enthusiasm than its ultimate production record ever justified.

However, the accuracy of postwar records is nowhere near as tight as the World War II material, especially at IHC, where production "discipline" seemingly bordered on chaos. Thus, what most "date charts" of postwar vintage do is take contract length, divide by months, and come up with approximate dates. Even so, barrel dates and even makers often line up only very loosely. So here I've included "durations" and allow you to do the math, in concert with the gross production chart on p. 101 of *The Complete M1 Garand*. And where I have been able to pin down some data that would be of use to collectors and researchers, I've included appropriate notes.

Again, none of the following data should be seen as ironclad rules. Guidelines, perhaps . . .

- 1952–54: SA batch 4200001 to 4399999

- 1953–54: IHC batch 4400000 to 4660000

- 1953–54: H&R (HRA code) batch 4660001 to 4800000 (unassigned: 4800001-4999999)

- August 1952: SA "NATO" standard batch 5000000 to 5000500, out of sequence, apparently intended for European subcontractors/armed forces

- Mid-1954-56: IHC batch 5000501–5278245

- 1954-55: SA batch 5278246–5488246

- 1954-56: H&R (HRA) batch 5488247–5793847

4.65 million IHC gap letter receiver.

A 4.68 million H&R rifle.

- 1955–57: SA batch
  5793848–6099905

From August 1956 to early 1957, an H&R "blip" batch was reassigned from the Springfield batch to H&R for a 400- to 500-rifle contract overrun. (I have seen four of these, one with an HRA 7.62x51 barrel, the others with rather odd, but apparently original, earlier H&R tubes in conventional .30 caliber.

Interesting Subgroups

The receivers ranging from 4440000 to well over 4445000 were International Harvesters actually produced in 1953 by Springfield Armory.

The receivers ranging from 4638XXX to about 4660000 were the "gap letter" "IHC" receivers, actually produced at Springfield in 1953–54. Likewise for those ranging from 5198034 to 5213034, in about 1955–56.

No precise numbers exist for the receivers bearing IHC logos actually built at H&R, but the range in which these are sometimes found includes 5213035 to somewhat over 5217000. This was also 1955–56, and apparently some of these originally bore "HRA" barrels.

As a group, M1Cs are postwar modifications of wartime receivers in the range 3200000 to 3800000. A few doubtful Winchesters exist, with nominal chance of authenticity. But those with the highest possibility of authentic provenance would be those that coordinate precisely in the same production time frame.

A 1954 "competition" SA receiver in the 5.2 million range, on the left, and an IHC ca. 1953–54 in the 4.52 million range.

A 5.63 million H&R, received from the CMP with all H&R parts save the bolt, a condition very quickly rectified.

M1Cs are wartime receivers that saw virtually exclusive postwar use and are therefore "original" in what would ordinarily be a "rebuilt" kind of configuration.

Such lists are necessarily incomplete. However, they help explain things like the recently observed IHC parts cache I inspected, all of which bore heavy, characteristic greenish phosphate over fairly heavy pitting. International Harvester had bad quality control problems, which apparently horrified military inspectors and the armory, and I have seen misground receiver contours, among other faults, on IHCs. Still, they are fascinating to collectors because of the many permutations and variations. And it is a testament to Garand's engineering skills that the rifle would still work, and rather well, grossly out of specification and beyond the mundane parameters of even a mediocre craftsman.

All contractors produced spare parts as well as receivers and complete rifles. And we continue to run into anomalies: SA barrels on H&R receivers, of precisely the right date and apparently undisturbed; LMR barrels and HRA barrels in similar places; and so on. I recall reading Dave McClain on some subject or other in the GCA newsletter saying, "Never say never," and while I won't go out on a limb and suggest that all such rifles were delivered that way, I'm not foolish enough to say the opposite, either! Not too long ago I handled a very nice, very late International Harvester rifle in virtually mint condition, whose owner was a veteran. He had owned the rifle since 1960 and had a bill of sale. The barrel bore the earliest date I have ever seen on an "LMR," and he asked me at the end of our conversation, "Is it right?" I said, "It's great!" Which it was. Anything else I'd told him would have been guesswork.

PART 2

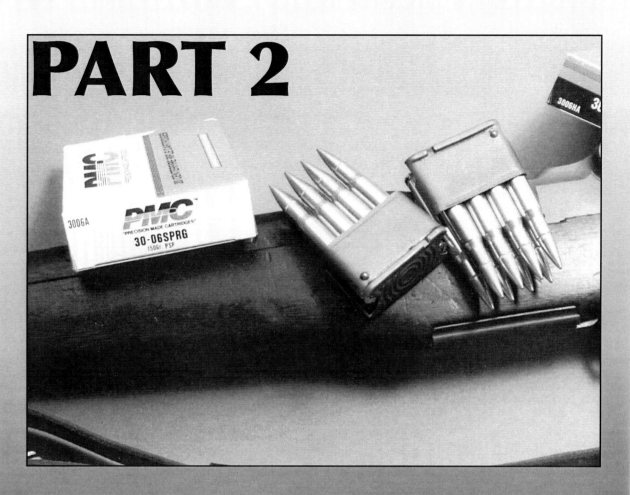

PART 2

COLLECTING AND SHOOTING THE M1 GARAND IN THE NEW MILLENNIUM: MYSTERIES SOLVED, TROUBLE AVOIDED, TARGETS HIT

It's hardly amazing that a mere tool becomes almost a cult object. Look what happened with cutlery, plates, vintage cars, the Jeep, and even bottles. The M1, of course, is still used for its main purposes: precision shooting and training in the general discipline of firearms responsibility. A couple of my friends think M1s are just plain ugly, and I don't dispute that, either. To me, they look precisely the way a rifle ought to look, and I wax mine and clean them just about every time I think of it. Indeed, when *The Complete M1 Garand* finally hit the market in 1998, I had spent so much money preparing that tome that I'd sold every rifle I owned just to make ends meet. Since then, I've slowly built up a stock of rifles, mainly from the proceeds of

that book. I therefore appreciate them more than ever before.

This part of *The Classic M1 Garand* is about enjoying and maintaining the rifle and, incidentally, making sure your thumbs (based on my mail, some of you have far more than two) and your face remain fairly intact—that is, SAFETY!

There isn't much here about ammunition and reloading (most of that was covered in the previous volume), though I have included some updates.

And we'll address the touchiest parts of maintaining and smoothing the rifle in detail, with some fairly controversial but nearly foolproof procedures.

CHAPTER 6
ANSWERS TO M1 PUZZLES FOUND IN THE MAIL AND ELSEWHERE

When I was teaching adult education back in Wisconsin, now some 21 long years ago, I appreciated the many and varied questions the students asked because they kept me on my toes and active in the fields in which I taught. But, boy—when you write a book, some days it's like a barrage! On top of that, the articles I've published in *Gun World*, various *Guns and Ammo* annuals, *GUNS*, and some of Cowle's history magazines have generated tons of correspondence. What this chapter will do is pluck out some of those queries that are of general interest (usually ones I got repeatedly) and relay the answers here for your perusal.

Frankly, I dislike the "Q&A" format used in magazines (even the ones I've written myself), because what they mostly do is let a writer pick and choose based on the information at his fingertips. So what you'll find here is combinations of questions I've been asked, and in some cases I can only cast a little light on them. As for those aspects that I fail to address, I suggest that someone else may want to do a little research, for which I lack both the time and means.

JOHN GARAND

People are perpetually asking me questions about John Garand the man, and I have precious little to contribute. The NRA's *The M1 Rifle* includes a thumbnail biography, and most of the other works in the bibliography of *The Complete M1 Garand* (p. 147) offer tidbits. Someone should do a combination technical/engineering and personal biography, because the brilliance I see in this rifle suggests a fascinating personality. But I never met the man.

What few papers of his I have seen indicate a very versatile mind, sharp wit, and a high order of broad-spectrum knowledge far beyond what we today think of as being stereotypical of engineers, often unfairly depicted as "nerds." He was apparently a tad eccentric as well and, at one point, had his living room reconfigured as a skating rink. Born in St. Remi, Quebec, Canada, in 1888, Garand had left Canada with his parents by the turn of the century. By age 20, he was a tool and gauge maker at Browne and Sharpe, and by 1914 he was acting foreman and machine designer for Federal Screw Corporation in Providence, Rhode Island.

Garand was in New York City during World War I, at which time he turned his talents to the design and development of firearms. He was intrigued with automatics' being subject to so many malfunctions. Soon after approaching the Naval Invention Bureau, he went to work for the National Bureau of Standards and developed a primer-actuated machine gun. Impressed by Garand's designs and detailed concepts, Army Ordnance moved him to the Springfield Armory in 1919.

Because of Army Ordnance interest in such systems—which always worked well under perfect conditions but never seemed to be reliable in the field—Garand's early designs employed primer activation systems, in which the primer actually initiates rearward action movement.

Most of these would not function without waxed or lacquered cartridge casings. Then, in 1925, the Army Ordnance Board discerned that conventionally prepared ammunition must be used in all new designs. By 1932, the Ordnance Board and Army Chief of Staff Douglas MacArthur ordered that any new designs must be chambered for the vast socks of caliber .30 Model of 1906 ammunition, much of which was of World War I or older Vintage. Garand's Rifle, Caliber .30 U.S., M1, was formally adopted by the U.S. Army on 9 January 1936.

It's when one gets into the details of the M1's firing mechanism that Garand's brilliance for detail is truly appreciated. Nothing very much like it—modular and complete—had been used before, and it has been flattered many times since by being endlessly copied in other designs. Unfortunately, as is the case with most American firearms designers—with the possible exceptions of William Ruger and John Browning—both John Garand and the greatness of his work seem to be, if not truly forgotten, then grossly underappreciated. Though he worked on some of the "T" series prototypes, he was never even consulted in the final phases of the design and production of the M14, and many ordnance officials were entirely too eager to suggest that the M1 and the later M14 were entirely unrelated, and even to imply that Garand was only peripherally involved in either project. This ridiculous bit of fraud must have left a bitter taste in Garand's mouth, but apparently he said nothing. I, for one, doubt whether the M14 would have had anywhere near the terrible teething troubles it did had Garand been directly involved. And the rifle might have been a little sturdier.

Garand died on February 16, 1974, at age 86.

I am not a biographer, and I lack the means to research Garand anyway. Although I do not intend to remain in Arizona one instant longer than necessary, my next major move will be only about halfway to the East Coast, which is where such work would have to be done. And, really, we're all some 26 years late . . . perhaps at least 50 years too late.

BAYONETS AND BLADES

M1 accessories, all by themselves, have become an independent collecting field, and although I try to avoid getting deeply into accessories, there are some that are both functional and decorative.

The 10-pocket "Mills"-type ammunition belt with snap pockets—of any vintage from the turn of the century (i.e., 19th to 20th) to recent Korean and Chinese copies—is extremely handy. The latest "copies" do not include grommet holes for hanger accessories and work just as well. In fact, as you read this, I have Scotchgarded one for regular range use. The one pictured with the accessories in *The Complete M1 Garand* (photo 46, p. 83) dates from 1916, belonged to a "China Station" marine in the late 1930s through the late 1940s, and apparently saw service in both world wars, as did the bayonet (the blade, anyway—more about that, later).

M1s eventually saw use with webbing slings, but mostly long after World War II. I have been looking for 40 years, and I have never seen a shot of a World War II American soldier or marine who was anywhere near combat using anything but a M1907 leather sling or variant thereof, and I've seen very few shots of other slings in the hands of combat troops as late as the Korean conflict.

Though web slings were produced, they never seem to have been issued to fighting units. One old gyrene told me, "Them rag slings, they'd fray and tear and rot and stink. Let the boots have 'em!" And that's apparently what the services did.

M1907 slings in military service used brass or steel hooks and hardware, with heavy rivets securing the hooks and flax stitching securing the keepers. The list of known contractors is vast, and I have purchased from government stocks slings made by at least 20 manufacturers—some of them obviously "off-the-shelf" commercial items that met the general specification. Thus, almost any sling of the correct type and age may actually have been in issue during World War II. Most of

A super M1 bearing one of Leslie Tam's extra-heavy custom M1907 slings.

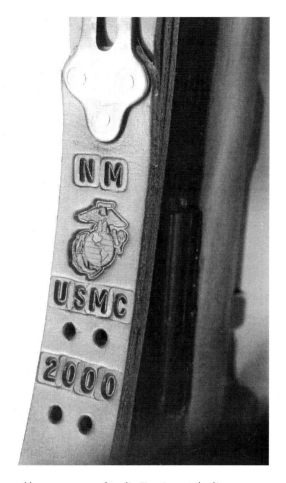

Close-up of logos on one of Leslie Tam's match slings.

these run very dark in color—reddish to deep brown, especially if oiled—and are physically lighter than their World War I counterparts. The steel fittings were a World War II revision; all others used brass exclusively, blackened by various means.

My favorite slings for my most pampered rifles are made by Leslie Tam in Honolulu, incorporating some vintage hardware along with some new fixtures on very heavy leather, and my Beretta now sports a match style, with numbered hole settings and is emblazoned with the Marine Corps anchor and globe. Why, you might ask, put something like that on an *Italian* rifle, of all things? One area where sophisticated collectors and I agree is this: a good part of the fun in accumulating these wonderful toys is appreciating the cosmopolitan nature of their use and adoption.

Many manufacturers can provide commercial or high-quality clones of the M1907-style sling, and at very reasonable prices. There are some very white, dry "military" M1907s marked "MRT" with which I have had problems in the field. Two of them have broken on me. Since I use slings both as carrying straps and shooting aids, I *hate* when that happens. These are around for sale at sensible prices, but I have decided not to purchase any more because sooner or later I will drop a rifle and break something, and then I will be furious.

Bayonets are nice display accessories, though prices are going steadily upward, especially for GI items. Southern Ohio Guns apparently still has, at this writing, the entire Danish supply of U.S. 10-inch bayonets, both the M1 and the M1905E1 shortened 10-incher.

71

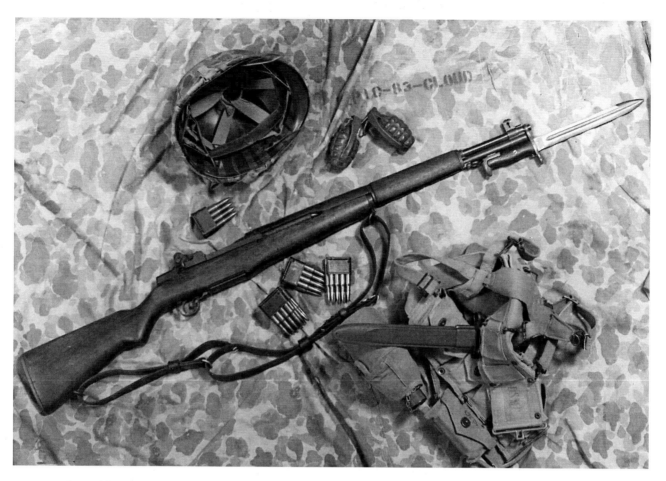

An M1 with World War II memorabilia, including a M1905E1 bayonet and a ca. 1916 Mills cartridge belt, which apparently saw service in both world wars.

With the exception of the late M5 and M5A1 bayonets, based on the carbine design and whose blade configuration is still standard with all U.S. military bayonets, *any* bayonet designed for the '03 Springfield fits the M1 and is at least nominally appropriate.

However, virtually any bayonet used on the M1 after 1936, even if built in 1905, would have been phosphated ("Parkerized") and fitted with black plastic grips. Original M1905s were used with the M1 so configured, and wartime production of the 16-inch M1905 (usually called, unofficially, the "model of 1942") was the same basic hunk of steel. Shortened versions of either are usually referred to as "M1905E1," and very few of the wartime production lot were ever shortened.

A gas trap rifle or any rifle below roughly 150,000 would be most appropriately fitted with a retrofinished M1905 of the full 16-inch configuration, though, of course, this doesn't mean such arms were always issued that way during World War II. And a study of World War II photographs reveals that 10- and 16-inch blades were issued throughout the war, any given unit usually having *all* of the same length, with only airborne units actually getting any preference, their needs calling for the 10-inchers almost exclusively due to space considerations on aircraft.

The 10-inch bayonets are referred to as "M1" bayonets, even though many were also issued with the earlier Springfield '03 and the contemporary '03A3.

A little analysis is called for here. People are forever telling me they have difficulty keeping their bayonets sharp, even used with self-sharpening sheaths. There's logic to this.

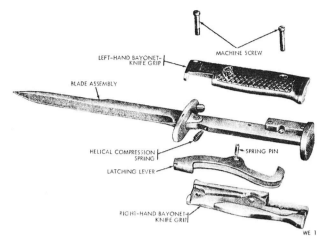

LEFT-HAND BAYONET-KNIFE GRIP

BLADE ASSEMBLY

MACHINE SCREW

HELICAL COMPRESSION SPRING

LATCHING LEVER

SPRING PIN

RIGHT-HAND BAYONET-KNIFE GRIP

WE 1

Figure 5-45. Disassembly/assembly of bayonet-knife M5A1.

Exploded view of the original M5 from U.S. Army Training Manual 9-1005-222-35. The M5 series bayonet was the only blade ever designed specifically and exclusively for the M1. The M5A1 is much more common.

Closeup of a standard postwar gas cylinder/sight assembly, with "high hump" gas cylinder lock and standard front sight.

Unusual rear view of an IHC front sight on what is obviously a postwar gas cylinder. Note: "overhang" on both sides of sight.

Until recently, bayonets were never intended to be cutting instruments, and they were *not* knives, despite their physical resemblance. They are *spearpoints*, to be handled and manipulated and used as spearpoints. That is the theory, anyway, behind their rather relaxed heat treatment. If bayonets held an edge and were used as they were supposed to be, a lot more soldiers would have a lot more scars and missing digits. Traditional bayonets can be used for some hacking functions and moderate prying, but if hardened to a true knife specification—as were some early "M1942s"—there is a tendency for the blade to break, especially at the 16-inch length.

Of the last generation of bayonets for the M1 rifle were the M5 and M5A1, which do not have a loop in the hilt that fits on the muzzle of the barrel but rather a stub that goes into the gas cylinder lock screw. These can still be had for sensible prices, and they are, in fact, the first generation of standard-issue bayonet blades from their inception designed to actually be used as knives.

The M5A1 was produced by many makers and in several different countries. The same "scabbard, bayonet-knife, M8A1" and its successors fit this blade and virtually every other U.S. bayonet produced since about 1948, and a lot of others as well. If, for some goofy reason, you feel compelled to shoot your M1 with a bayonet fixed, you are in for some surprises. Most service rifles shoot better, and with considerably less felt recoil, with the blade mounted. This is *not* true of match-prepared rifles, except for the recoil reduction, which is a simple matter of the physics of the center of gravity. The M5 series is far more modern, sporting a large release/latch lever and tab, but has nowhere near the romance and panache of the much larger World War II blades. However, it is a much more utilitarian knife and is actually convenient around the house. I have just located a Beretta M5A1 and was amazed to find that the same owner had a 10-inch Beretta-made and marked "M1" bayonet, which I did not previously know had ever been produced outside the United States.

In Korea, the Philippines, and Taiwan, the longer bayonet blades were reconfigured to the M5/M5A1 profile, apparently for convenience, and many of these are on the market at relatively bargain prices as of this writing.

GAS CYLINDERS AND SIGHTS

Several of the photos of M1 "business ends" in *The Complete M1 Garand* were intended to give a general idea what correct hardware of various vintages looks like. However, I didn't want those captions to become books in and of themselves, so I explained most of the detail in the text. Here I'll be a little more specific. The rather more obviously "bent ear" front sights are IHCs and Winchesters and look a great deal alike. International Harvesters are nominally 15/16 inch from extreme outward measurement to extreme outward measurement; Winchesters—which, if not refinished are usually virtually black—measure 13/16 inch in the same plane (although, I hasten to add, enough sand blasting and refinishing will change these approximate measurements considerably). Virtually all other M1 front sights from all other sources will be very close to 11/16 inch unless they have been damaged or crushed.

Just below the sight, the "straddle" measurement across the dovetail, on the gas cylinder, over which the sight slides when it's

being fitted, is 1/2 inch for the early gas port-style gas cylinders and approximately 19/32 inch for all late-war and postwar units in the same area. One can see this difference. If the dovetail hangs out to the left and right of the sight, it's a late style; if flush with the sight base, it's the early style. The late style is probably stronger, but the reason for the change was to provide greater front-end windage adjustment without having to radically modify anything else in the rifle.

Winchester gas cylinders are virtually all of the "early" configuration and can be spotted because the flat on the rear "hoop"—the upper one that contacts or comes very close to the handguard ferrule—is either off center or not there at all. This is true of some early Springfields and some gas cylinders that were sanded too severely in rebuilding. The Winchester cylinder also has no beveled "toe" on the bayonet lug underneath the operating rod tube, in contrast to all others. Virtually all World War II Springfield gas cylinders and most Winchesters will bear small hardness punch marks, usually on the bayonet lug's bottom surface, and these appear in random numbers and depths. The small letters that appear on all sorts of Springfield cylinders, even many postwar units, are the leftovers from various finish experiments intended to develop a better, more durable finish for the big stainless-steel part, which, in service, tended to become bright metal fairly quickly and caused complaints almost immediately from the field. The final solution, as nearly as I can tell from microscopic analysis, seems to have been some kind of black-chrome-related plating (very dark), which appeared on many very late rifles. But I do not know for sure if this, too, was merely a refined experiment applied in rebuilding or if it was being done at the armory. In any case, this process seems to have produced an extremely durable finish.

All Italian gas cylinders carry the maker's letter code mark, although, interestingly, I have seen at least two gas cylinders that were definitely American-made and wartime carrying the "PB" identifier. One of these was

Fulton Armory barrel in .30-06, basically an enhanced GI specification unit.

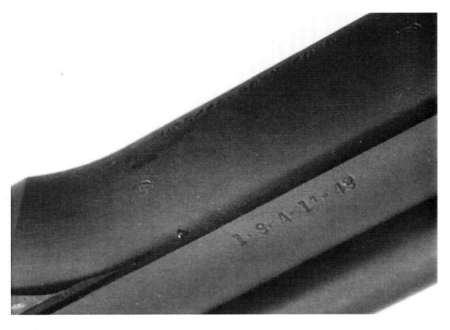

A Springfield Armory (U.S.) barrel from November 1943, found still attached to its original receiver on a CMP rifle the author received recently.

on a DCM-supplied WIN-13 and seems to have been the original gas cylinder for the rifle, which I suspect—but cannot prove—was rebuilt or refinished and inspected at Beretta at some time or other.

AUTHENTICITY AND PERIPHERALS

I am forever being asked about the use of terms like "correct," "original," and "authentic," with regard to restorations, and although I will not go into a lot of the specifics here, I will explain some economics and try to give some practical data.

Anyone who thinks that a great deal of money can be made by restoring rifles should think again. It can be done—usually by luck and diligent, patient scrounging— but it is not easy. My projects along those lines have almost always lost money, and generally a lot of it. There are some scoundrels out there who will modify existing parts, remark civilian barrels, and resort to welding and reconfiguration in an effort to produce something that, if not downright dishonest and fraudulent, is certainly questionable.

Yet there are situations in which a serious collector needs a specific example to complete his array and has no choice. Much against my better judgment, I recently agreed to help a correspondent in bringing a four-digit M1 back to its fully "original" gas trap configuration. This would have been incredibly stupid to even start, except that he had discovered a gas cylinder, intact, complete with its original sights, screws, and all fittings, and his rifle had *already* been rebuilt to gas port configuration in September 1940 and apparently hadn't been touched since. In other words, with perhaps $700 out of pocket, he was very close and needed only a barrel and the original handguard ferrule, which turned out to be rather easy to find.

Probably the best advice I gave him was not to fool with his original vintage 1940 tube from the gas port conversion rebuild, since it is and was one of the earliest gas port barrels extant, but to have a brand-new barrel made from a Douglas blank. By the way, most 1940 barrels were not dated by the usual stamping, although they're easy enough to spot. But this one—which was verifiably authentic—had the usual markings of that time and was marked "9-40" (very large, perpendicular to everything else, and above the chamber, of all places). I have seen a couple of other barrels, all early, with similarly emblazoned dates in large letters—including one on a Winchester (though 180 degrees flip-flopped from what he described) *under* the handguard. This is very uncommon. One collector suggested that these barrels were dated by inspectors on some selection basis, probably just one per heat-treatment lot, before the rationalized manufacture dating system was put in place. This makes some sense but is merely logic, not evidence. Point is, if you see it, don't panic—it seems to be what I have learned to call "extraneous/peripheral" markings (or, if you like my original term, "mystery marks"), the purpose of which was forgotten, most likely, before the first soldier held the rifle but which have been observed too many times to be illegitimate.

You see, fakery is the attempt to profit by ascribing artificial value to an object. "Mystery marking" is just stuff applied for some short-term purpose and should have no meaning at all, except as an interesting footnote.

I stressed to my correspondent that if I were to be associated with his rifle in any way, although I had no objections to his putting parts together, I wanted no one to think that barrel was original and authentic, save perhaps from a few yards away. This was very neatly solved. The smith who installed the barrel used no right-side barrel markings at all except the crossed cannons, but of nonregulation size, and put the ACTUAL DATE OF INSTALLATION parallel with the bore, along with the owner's initials, at 6 and 12 o'clock locations. This rifle won't change hands, barring some terrible

tragedy, for the next quarter-century or so, and the 1940 tube is still on hand. But this is a case of luck and providence.

Elaborate restorations, especially of early M1s and Winchesters, almost never work out financially, unless one is just a few parts away. A friend's CMP H&R came along in the middle of 1999, and it was complete and correct, save for a Winchester bolt. Guess what! That Winchester bolt didn't live there very long!

But trying to pull together a full-house restoration, especially of an early World War II rifle with nothing actually in hand save the receiver is an expensive nightmare, and correct, original, cartouched buttstocks, in particular, have become brutally expensive. Barrels are often a monstrous stumbling block. It was my original intention, by the way (since so many fake and "modified" barrels are floating around these days), to measure and hardness-test a rather huge batch of barrels and present the results here. This proved to a be a fool's errand because, even among authentic specimens of similar vintage, there are tiny changes in machining style—placement of certain curves and so on—such that it would have amounted to a great deal of work to accomplish nothing. But there is an alternative for the collector with access to a smith's takeoff barrels and some that are basically elaborate tent stakes: examine all the specimens possible with a micrometer, look for tool mark patterns, and compare all to specimens on the market. Be always on the lookout for places on barrels that seem to be too thin, turned, flattened, overstamped, or filed . . . a good trick is to roll a barrel on a hard, flat surface and look for wobbles and bumps. Use an 8- to 10-power magnifying loupe, and look very, very closely at markings and surface eccentricities.

To shooters, it's all much easier. . . . Check throat, muzzle, and shoot. . . .

USING AND SMOOTHING THE CIVILIAN M1

Your rifle is no longer in military service. It's yours, in the traditional capitalist sense of the term. Hopefully, it's fought its last firefight.

The M1's ejector and spring assembly, almost ready for final polish.

Bolt face of the M1 Garand, with the author's center punch testing extractor tension. The already polished extractor lies just below.

Yet, without converting your rifle to something else or substantially altering its unique looks or basic functions, you, like most shooters, want it to perform well.

The firing mechanism and bolt of the M1 are two of Garand's areas of triumph, but your applications for them are not quite the same as those contemplated some 70 years ago. The M1 characteristically flips brass much farther from the rifle than is convenient for a civilian shooter who wants to recycle his brass—and spews it all over the place, too. In combat, it's a good idea to get brass out from underfoot and out of the immediate position.

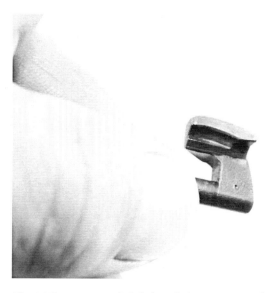

The M1's extractor, slightly beveled to M14 specification, ready for touch-up.

The M1's extractor is very positive and quite massive and has a tendency, especially when not clean, to "ding" the occasional case rim. Again, this was a military rifle, and brass condition after firing was well down the list of priorities. Clearing the chamber, though, was imperative.

These problems are easily solved.

We'll start with the bolt. Once it has been removed, study the extractor surfaces that contact the cartridge rim and test the tension on the ejector with your finger. Take a look at the photos of the ejector (top left) and extractor (top right), and briefly study the photo at left, which shows the bolt face with both the ejector and extractor in place. Don't take anything apart yet.

You're going to need at least the following, and save everything for the trigger work, too:

- A punch or M1 tool or both, or an old screwdriver you don't plan to use for screws anymore

- The finest steel wool you can get

- At least one spare ejector and spring

- Probably some thin cutting oil or other surface lubricant for use with the abrasives below

- A collection of flat, mild abrasives (stones, very mild files, even emery boards will do, nothing coarser than 220 grit, preferably no coarser than 400)

- A bottle of cold blue, the directions to which you should follow whenever you're removing surface finish—not to fool anybody, but to provide some corrosion resistance where bare metal has been exposed (you'll use this during the trigger work, too)

- A few sheets of emery paper, the wet and dry kind, of 220 and about 400 grit

- Whatever collection of paper towels, brushes, soap, hand cleanser, and/or scouring powder you find handy for cleaning yourself and your tools, parts, and rifle

- Toothpicks, pipe cleaners, mild wet abrasives (automotive polishing compound is handy), some small brushes, and perhaps also a high-quality dental pick

- About +3 or +4 diopter viewing glasses or an 8- or 10-power magnifying loupe for viewing parts close up (simple magnifying glasses are generally *not* adequate)

- A spare firing pin (also a good idea, regardless of this procedure)

In particular, note the "dip" or detent just over one-third of the way back on the ejector body. That little depression has to line up with the shaft on the extractor for the bolt to go together, meaning the spring ejector has to be depressed during disassembly. Before tearing down the bolt, again study the extractor *in situ*, and note the contact surfaces. Those are the ones you're going to polish.

We're illustrating here from the military manual the disassembly technique using the fixture (see p. 82). If you have this device, great! Chances are you don't, so remember that this happens fast and that the ejector leaves in a hurry, so always aim the bolt face into a bucket

Center punch aligned with extractor at bottom of bolt, ejector depressed, almost ready for removal. It's wise to aim the ejector someplace safe, preferably where it can be found.

or restrain the ejector like grim death. The M1 tool carries on its arm a semieliptical projection designed to compress the ejector precisely to the right depth and restrain its path out, and that's a good shortcut. An empty cartridge with the same base as .45 ACP or a little smaller is very handy. Finally, after some 37 years, I am actually able to disassemble and even assemble the M1 bolt once in a while with nothing more than my bare hands and a center punch. But I don't rely on doing that, and you may not have 37 years to learn. *Everything* depends on the alignment of that little slot, and it will stay stable only under pressure, albeit pressing in on the extractor will tend to slightly realign it if you're close enough.

Before beginning, assess your mechanical skills. Many people find it easier to strip the bolt in a vise, and I have also seen homemade fixtures. Watch what you're doing, read and reread the instructions, and proceed with the tear-down when you have plenty of time. It's the reassembly that's awkward. Don't even think about using power tools, and if you have problems with mechanical functions in general, pack up the whole thing and take it to your gunsmith.

Using your driver, punch, or M1 tool, compress the ejector the appropriate depth; aim the bolt face someplace safe, keeping pressure on the ejector throughout; push or drive the extractor out toward the top of the bolt (as illustrated in the photo at left); and, as gently as you can, ease out the other parts, including the firing pin and the extractor spring/spring plunger.

Much of the rest is instinct and analysis. So again, before applying *any* tools or abrasives, go back and study the photos and illustrations. Generally, nothing is done with the extractor spring/extractor spring plunger assembly except to clean it up and put a little grease in its detent before reassembly. If your eyesight is not perfect for close-up work, get yourself an 8- to 10-power loupe and study the parts, looking for burrs, pits, stuck-on bits of filth, abrasions, and tool marks. It is common to snip one or two coils off the ejector spring, then restretch it, especially in .308, before reassembly. (I only do this if I know from experience that a rifle chambered for the shorter cartridge is tossing brass way too far.) Then meticulously clean *everything* (preferably working with the tiny parts in a strainer if you do this in a sink with water) and again look for flaws and abrasions of any sort.

The easiest part is flat and simple, and that's the firing pin. Check the tip for anything unusual, and if it's sharp enough to cut your skin or in any way convoluted, do not hesitate—replace it *immediately!* Firing-pin eccentricities contribute to the slamfire phenomenon (discussed later), and the nose is what actually strikes the primer. Check the long span for signs of cracks or fractures, and if you see a line but can't determine whether it's a crack or not, the next step should help clarify things. (If the firing pin does prove to be cracked, replace it *immediately!*)

Now, we go to work on the pin, and this is easy. You're going to polish it until the sides show no tool marks; you don't have to be able to comb your hair with it, but every tool mark is a potential snag at some time in the rifle's life; get rid of them, and that life will be longer and safer. Cold blue the shiny parts.

You'll want to spray some kind of Teflon spray into the bolt's detent after you have flushed, cleaned, and done what you can to inspect that raceway. Or you can use a tiny

touch of grease on either side of the pin when you do the reassembly.

Now take another long, slow look at your ejector and spring assembly (refer back to the top left-hand photo on p. 77); grab some pipe cleaners (and/or toothpicks if you're particularly industrious) and make that spring shine like chrome plate (or as close as you can get), preferably inside and out; and moderately deburr the ejector itself using automotive polishing compound, steel wool, and rags. DON'T EVEN THINK ABOUT CHANGING CONTOURS ON THE EJECTOR, ESPECIALLY THE RIDGE! (I do this while watching TV— almost like absent-mindedly whittling, often for several hours.) Then clean the parts carefully with brushes and dry. All metal filings must be removed before reassembly (avoid using emery paper or files on this part). And again, reblue and lubricate the channel before reassembly.

The extractor won't be changed much either, but because the finish process often results in tiny phosphate inclusions on the extractor that cause it to abrade brass, you're basically just going to remove some finish and any obvious tool marks, *very gently*, in the areas where the cartridge touches or is likely to touch the part. You don't want *any* lube on the exterior of the extractor, but you can clean that up, if necessary, after reassembly.

It's a good idea to use this opportunity to clean up the bolt face. Don't try to remove pits; if they are there and they offend you, replace the bolt and check your headspace. But do remove any blobs of material stuck there—they *do* get stuck there, more than anywhere else in the rifle, at 50,000 pounds of pressure per shot —and degrease, then use cold blue to at least slightly control corrosion.

You can also check firing-pin protrusion, if you have the military gauges or other adequate precision measuring tools, and the repair standards table on the next page provides safety-related measurements.

Also, while your rifle is disassembled, without the springs and operating rod, put your bolt back in the receiver and, preferably using

CHAPTER 7

REPAIR STANDARDS

7-1. General

The repair standards included h e r e i n give the minimum and maximum measure-ments of repaired parts; those beyond the limits will be replaced by new parts.

7-2. Specific

a. Bolt Assembly.

Fig. No.	Point of Measurement	Repair Standards	
		Minimum	Maximum
5-17.	Firing pin protrusion	0.044 in.	0.060 in. (overseas)

b. Gas Cylinder Group.

Fig. No.	Point of Measurement	Repair Standards	
		Minimum	Maximum
5-23.	Gas cylinder bore	0.5320 in.	—

c. Follower Group.

Fig. No.	Point of Measurement	Repair Standards	
		Minimum	Maximum
5-14.	Operating rod gas piston diameter	0.525 in.	—

d. Trigger Housing Assembly.

Fig. No.	Point of Measurement	Repair Standards	
		Minimum	Maximum
5-5.	Trigger-trigger pull	*M1* 5.5 lb	7.5 lb
		M1C and M1D (Sniper's) 4.5 lb	6.5 lb

e. Barrel and Receiver Group.

Fig. No.	Point of Measurement	Repair Standards	
		Minimum	Maximum
5-31.	Throat of chamber	0.306 in. (overseas)	0.310 in. (hands of troops)
5-32.	Barrel gas port	0.5991 in. outer (over-seas)	

Repair Standards table from U.S. Army TM 9-1005-222-35.

feeler gauges, check the lug clearances, wiggle the bolt around, and study its movement. Worn, peened, and improperly machined bolts, especially in the lug areas, are both a safety and a wear problem. Look for excessive play.

If you haven't already lost your ejector, you still may in the reassembly process. Be sure you get the extractor spring/plunger assembly in properly, mash down on the ejector with whatever contrivance you have at hand, and, following the steps in the illustration on p. 82, reassemble your bolt.

If you are conservative, relaxed, use no power tools, and keep everything clean and spiffy, this process cannot harm your rifle and should treat your brass much better. Sometimes, though, another condition—say, excessive gas in the system due to a corroded port—may cause brass to be slam-danced into oblivion and badly beaten, but at least now you should eventually be able to find it.

By the way, it's a good idea to prepare a spare ejector and firing pin to keep on hand, particularly if you have more than one rifle.

Since we discussed firing pin protrusion and so forth, by the way, some of the more commonly used specifications from the repair standards table are presented on p. 80. You need to know, though, that some civilian gas cylinders and, therefore, pistons, have larger bores and that civilian barrel throats usually use much gentler leades and throats; the figures here apply to GI units only.

SMOOTH, RELIABLE, DURABLE: THE BRILLIANT M1 FIRING MECHANISM AND HOW TO DO A TRIGGER JOB WHERE YOU ALMOST CAN'T BREAK ANYTHING

The M1's firing mechanism has several fascinating characteristics, of which perhaps the best is that it is *very* easy to employ both a "service" trigger and a "match" trigger on the same rifle, interchanging them in less time than it takes to explain how to yank down the trigger guard, which, as covered in *The Complete M1 Garand*, is where field-strip begins. It contains not just the trigger, but the hammer/striker, sear/disconnector, and safety mechanisms, as well as (snapped into the housing itself) the clip ejector. And the whole apparatus, while not impervious to water or dirt, is a much better seal to the bottom of the mechanism than is found on most rifles of similar or later vintage.

I'm going to explain here a trigger-smoothing and slight lightening technique spun off of that described in the NRA's *The M1 Rifle*, and we'll employ virtually all the tools and supplies I detailed in the top-end, bolt-related job we just described and discussed.

Study the three photos in this section and the chart detailing the firing mechanism (p. 83). The chart is an illustration from the U.S. Army's rifle, national match, in its final version, and shows, from the top, a cocked trigger housing assembly on safe; a cocked unit, ready to fire, in match incarnation; and, at the bottom, a schematic and parts lexicon, in fired or ready-to-strip condition. OK, don't take yours apart yet, but take it out and play with it, studying the look and feel of the parts from all aspects. In particular, brace the hammer on its release, then press it back with the trigger still depressed and note how the sear/disconnector functions in various regimes, release the trigger once it's locked rearward, and so on.

Now, there are some things you need to know before going on. Many of these parts are very, very hard on their surface but much softer and more malleable below a few thousandths of an inch. We're removing *no* substantial amounts of material, simply cleaning up and polishing, then doing the same kind of lubrication and detail refinish we did in the last section. You'll need a few more doo-dads, too:

- Some pieces of 1/4-inch or slightly smaller dowel material or something similar, 4 to 7 inches long

- A set of feeler gauges that will allow you to measure any eccentricities that might cause you to reject a given firing mechanism that's out of true, or to try to adjust it

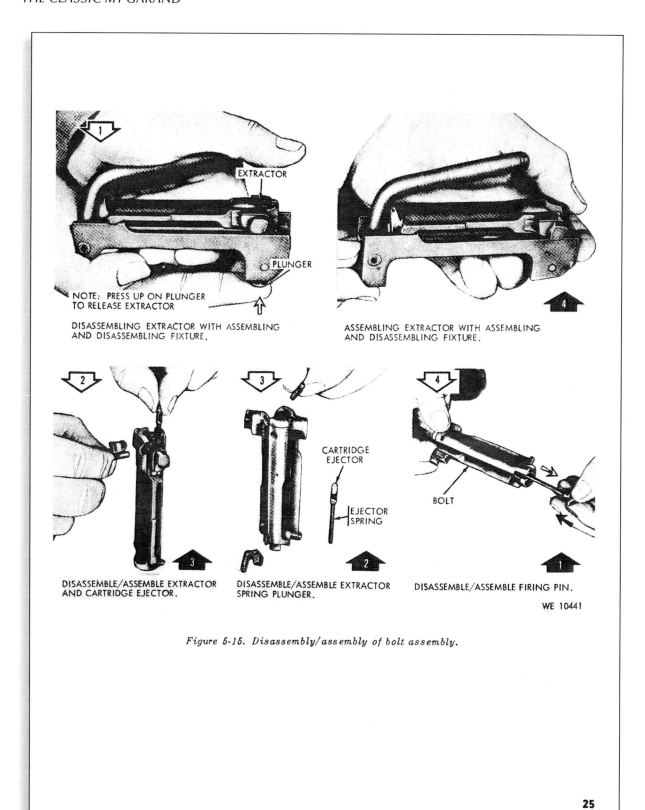

Figure 5-15. Disassembly/assembly of bolt assembly.

Procedure for disassembly and assembly of bolt, from U.S. Army TM 9-1005-222-35.

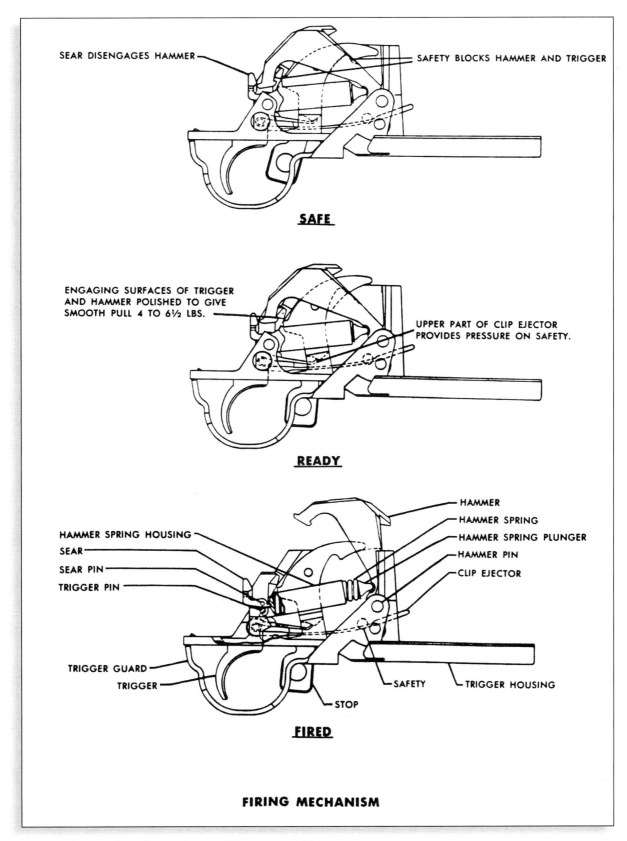

Firing mechanism chart, from U.S. Army TM 9-1005-222-35.

You might want to fix your housing in a vise to clean it up if it has visible burrs and machine marks, or use the securing holes to screw or peg it to a large wooden flat.

Let me briefly summarize, while you're looking at your housing and the drawings, what is ideally done.

The trigger/sear/disconnector assembly *will not be disassembled*, but some work (very little) will be done with *very mild* abrasives, some of it with the whole device in its fully assembled condition, if necessary; work will be done on all four surfaces, if required. The housing itself rarely needs any work, and the clip ejector need not be removed unless such work is required; study, watch, and listen for signs of grating and friction. All four hammer hook surfaces will be polished, but very tenderly. The safety may

require finish or burr removal, especially on the inside surface, but often does not. The hammer spring should be very nicely polished but not subjected to anything coarse at all. The hammer spring housing can be polished very bright inside, but be careful; this is very thin, brittle material, so work with oil and polishing compound and steel wool very slowly. Some people polish the nose of the hammer spring plunger to a bright finish, which does not affect trigger pull but supposedly has some impact on locking time; I usually don't bother unless I see some actual disruption.

No need to mess with the rest of the parts, unless something has happened. (See the illustration below for safety notes.)

Check for approximate parallelism at all locations of the hammer hooks. That is, you should not be able to measure any substantial

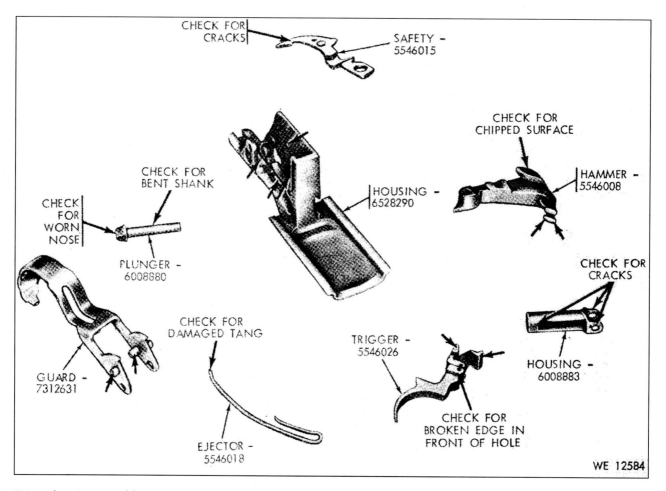

Trigger housing assembly inspection points, from U.S. Army TM 9-1005-222-35.

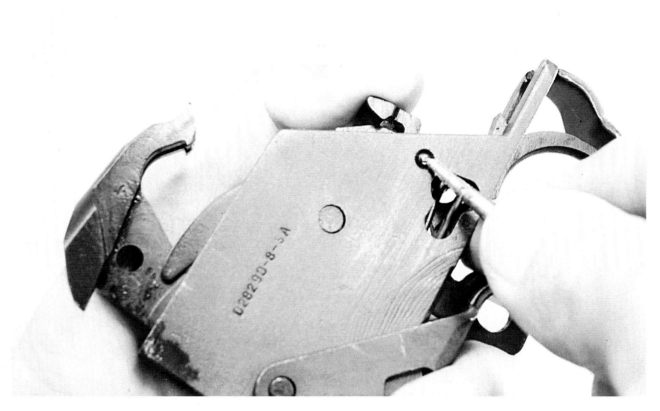

Driving the trigger pin out with a punch, trigger mechanism held forward, with the unit uncocked. Note burrs on the upper portion of the hammer, which proved not to cause friction or interference.

difference between the lock/friction points of front or rear, right or left engagement points in the "null," or cocked and ready. I have seen distorted and bent housings, which were truly unserviceable, but in particular, the trigger/sear/disconnector mechanism can be damaged very subtly such that it is out of parallel and must therefore be replaced. Indeed, it's not a bad idea at all to keep a spare hammer and trigger assembly or even a whole, fully assembled firing mechanism and/or a hammer and hammer spring housing on hand.

Overzealous filing, machine grinding, and attempts to remove too much material, especially on a part that's already defective, are the primary cause of parts failure in such a job. If you're one of those guys who can't wait to get out his big, old mill file, DON'T EVEN START ON THIS PROCESS!

Long before beginning, study the disassembly procedures (see the illustration on pp. 87–88) and the photo above. This photo shows the center punch actually beginning to dislodge the trigger pin, but, more important, it shows an early, extra-hole hammer that, on its upper center quadrant, contains some burrs and machine marks that *might* require the use of some polishing techniques. Whether it does or not (and it didn't, by the way) depends on the adjacent surfaces and clearances, which are highly individual. *Do not remove burrs that do not interfere with or touch anything.* Such removal might make things look nice, but it's wasted time. The photo above shows the same assembly, cocked, from the other side. Notice how tight the engagement is on this unit, which, ultimately, was only very tenderly polished.

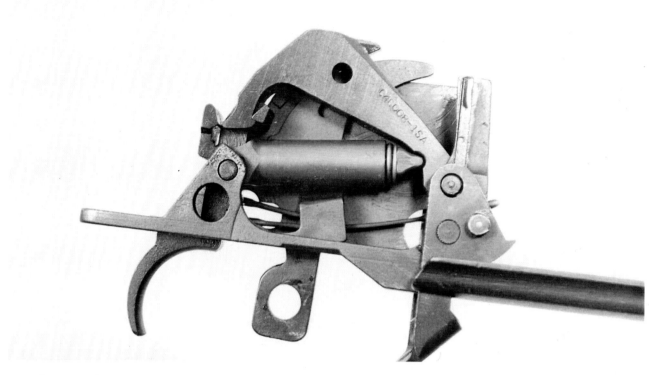

Complete trigger housing, viewed from right side, in cocked condition. Note the very tight front hammer hook fit and early -1 "extra hole" Springfield hammer and postwar "no ear" plunger head.

The photo on p. 89 is a little reminder for reassembly. Make *sure* the closed side of the hammer spring housing faces *outward* upon reassembly, and press forward and down or you may never get this nice "light through the hole" position required to start the trigger pin in its seated position.

Again, remember, you should find very few metal shavings, but they need to be removed and any bare metal touched up with cold blue and lubricated before reassembly. Regular inspection with your magnifying devices is absolutely imperative every few strokes or rubs of whatever polishing medium you have opted to use.

I do not suggest trying to make all the mating surfaces absolutely identical on the hammer hooks—and if you reconfigure anything, you are in trouble already. Again, this is detailed reburring, polishing, and touch-up.

I use stones to start, with oil or grease, if I have heavy burrs, moving quickly down to 400-grit emery, then to steel wool. A good portion of what causes scraping and grating in M1

triggers is the heavy phosphate, and once that's gone, it is amazing how nice a trigger can be. Indeed, as military rifles go, the M1 is almost always quite good.

I would not do these procedures on a true collector's rifle but would instead acquire an entirely separate firing mechanism, perhaps even of the same vintage "parts package," and set up a separate "shooting" trigger housing assembly/firing mechanism. But that's up to you.

Clumsy, overaggressive work here can cause all sorts of malfunctions in the M1, including random "machine gunning," slamfires, and failure to fire. Being a little too conservative simply means that one gets minimal improvement. I suggest—though it takes a very long time to work this way—assembling, disassembling, and testing the entire mechanism many times, doing a very moderate amount of work between each test period. This will help you learn the technique, too.

The main thing is to inspect constantly with the magnifier. When tiny traces of the finish are

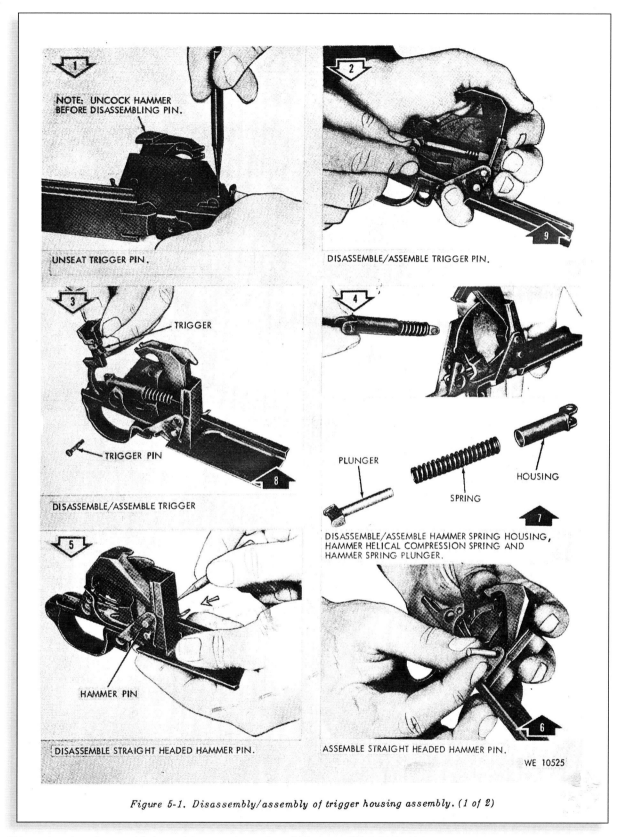

Figure 5-1. Disassembly/assembly of trigger housing assembly. (1 of 2)

Trigger housing disassembly/assembly procedures, from U.S. Army TM 9-1005-222-35.

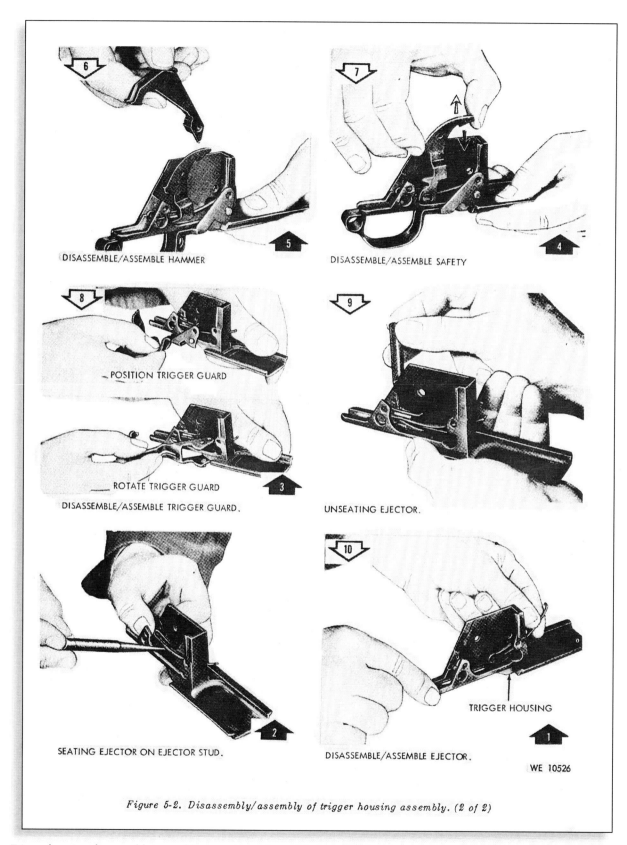

DISASSEMBLE/ASSEMBLE HAMMER

DISASSEMBLE/ASSEMBLE SAFETY

POSITION TRIGGER GUARD

ROTATE TRIGGER GUARD

DISASSEMBLE/ASSEMBLE TRIGGER GUARD.

UNSEATING EJECTOR.

SEATING EJECTOR ON EJECTOR STUD.

TRIGGER HOUSING

DISASSEMBLE/ASSEMBLE EJECTOR.

WE 10526

Figure 5-2. Disassembly/assembly of trigger housing assembly. (2 of 2)

Trigger housing disassembly/assembly procedures, from U.S. Army TM 9-1005-222-35.

Trigger mechanism ready to have the pin reinserted. Note that the clean hole is emerging, which can be seen through, and that the "closed" side of hammer spring housing is in the correct orientation.

everything else gleams, you are definitely done and maybe a little over the edge. And be particularly tender on the hammer hooks.

There is one procedure that J.B. Roberts suggests, which I have only used a couple of times and do not necessarily recommend. I include it here just in case you find it necessary to get where you have to. It's in the NRA's *The M1 Rifle*, quoted directly as follows. (Note that I use 400-grit where he uses 220-grit, and I check my work every couple of runs.)

> Take a 1 "x 8" strip of 220-grit, Wet or Dry or emery cloth, and insert it between the rear of the trigger and attached disconnector, abrasive side against the trigger. This is done with the trigger housing assembled, the hammer uncocked. Hammer spring tension in the assembly will hold the cloth in place. Making sure the abrasive surface touches only the trigger, slide the cloth back and forth, using about half the length of the strip. Check the weight of the pull about every fourth stroke until the trigger will hold . . . weight.

Roberts stressed the 4.5-pound weight, but I have been told that the current match standard is 4 pounds. Double-check if you're actually in competition, which, as of this writing, I'm not.

Many will find chalk, Prussian blue, and other marking mediums convenient for finding points of binding and abrasion. I find—and it may be experience or dumb luck—that I can usually find the sources of roughness by eyeball and hearing. Again, *constant* checking of polish levels with the magnifier is a fail-safe device and must be used.

At the first sign of deep bewilderment, overeagerness, or a deep desire to warm up the bench grinder or belt sander, take a walk. Then find your nearest armorer or smith who works on M1s, and have him do it. YOU ARE MAINLY REMOVING FINISH, *VERY* LITTLE METAL,

AND ONLY THE ACTUAL HIGH POINTS THAT CAUSE BINDING AND ABRASION IN THE MECHANISM.

Some shooters have had their entire trigger mechanism's internals (once set up) hard-chromed, and though I thought this was crazy at first, I have learned that it actually precludes wear, especially when coupled with heavy grease lubrication of the correct sort.

This mechanism is almost foolproof, which you should figure out from observation. If you go very slowly, inspect regularly, and have some mechanical skills, things are very unlikely to get messed up.

FUN AND SAFETY: AMMO AND AVOIDANCE OF DANGER

In the past couple of years, I've heard a lot of reference to "slamfire," a dangerous condition in which the Garand or any similar rifle discharges a round by movement of the bolt forward. Sometimes this results in a second round's discharging—and it can be catastrophic—when the bolt is not locked down and the operating rod fully forward.

Springfield Armory provided me with a copy of a Wayne Faatz article in *American Rifleman* (reprints of which can be ordered from the magazine). I will not reanalyze his or the NRA's data, save to point to improper detailed reloading procedure, softer than military-issue primers, case-sizing details, occasional case separation, and various glitches with firing pins and ejector modification. In fact, his article is part of the reason I no longer shorten ejector springs unless I have a definite problem. (He also notes that shooting glasses should be worn at all times, which I sometimes foolishly presume everyone does automatically.)

I do not disagree with any of his work or conclusions, but I do have something to add. I have seen two slamfires, or, rather, the remains from them, one in each of the popular calibers. The factor that I suspect is at the root of some of the problem—though by no means all of it—is

dirty or oily chambers, which, in a high-pressure rifle, especially a gas-operated one, can cause cases to stick on their way in or out and adhere in strange ways or places, even contributing to gross separations. This is called "hydraulic adhesion."

Both of the slamfire-caused specimens I saw had fallen victim to factory ammunition. I did some further calling and digging, and not a single one of the victims I contacted regularly used the standard chamber cleaning recommended by the military. This involves a chamber-cleaning brush with a patch over it, followed by the brush itself, cleaned completely of oil, with additional applications of absorbent patches. Oil especially, but also brass debris, powder fragments, and any foreign material must be removed and chamber polish maintained.

Commercial match barrels are usually very tightly chambered. This contributes to both accuracy and brass life. And, therefore, any foreign matter in the chamber means a cartridge's smoothness of entry and, therefore, speed is affected at the worst possible time. Oil here is a no-no.

Ammo

Federal has in its catalog a new version of 308GM using the 155-grain Palma Match bullet, though it is very unlikely this bullet will ever be loaded in .30/06 as a factory item. Sellier & Bellot has introduced a lot of very good ammunition in both calibers, and perhaps just as important, some of its "export" military format stuff in .308 is being sold at very sensible prices.

PMC/Eldorado has upgraded its whole ammunition line, including the 168-grain match bullets, as standard items in both chamberings.

Perhaps most important is that Sierra is offering virtually all its .30-caliber bullets in molycoated incarnations, and I've tested them and gotten wonderful results (partly covered elsewhere in this book). Most important of all, I can now say that molycoating and judicious cleaning of the M1 can at least double the useful life of an M1 Garand barrel, and probably do considerably more. I'm basing that

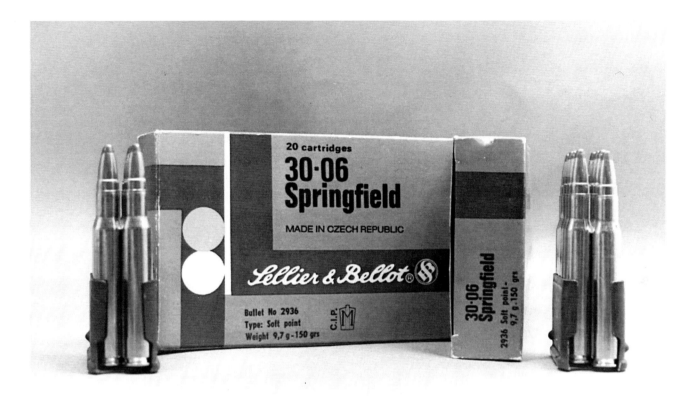

Sellier and Bellot .30-06.

on a barrel fired with only copper jackets, an identical one fired only with molycoated bullets, and the erosion generated after about 5,500 rounds. I'll know much more and publish the results within the next couple of years.

The Cold, Cold, Cold

I am also able to report that some of the unrelieved Citadel barrels (those that showed such machine stress that, when hot, they would shoot as many as 11 clicks left or right, and some of which were actually magnetic) have shown much improved performance via cryogenic treatment . . . that is, they actually shot where they were aimed! These units sold for as little as $50 in the period 1990–97 or so, and the very best of them were excellent. But they were graded. A couple of unscrupulous dealers unloaded what were effectively rejects through advertising and at gun shows, and so a great many of these flawed tubes are still sitting around waiting to surprise somebody.

Civilian "remanufactured" .30-06 on Lake City cases.

Radway Green .308, available from Century Arms.

Belted Israeli ball ammo, available from Navy Arms.

APPENDIX I
SOURCES

Perhaps the most useful publication for the Garand buff who wishes to immerse himself in this legendary firearm is the GCA Newsletter, from the Garand Collector's Association, P.O. Box 7498, North Kansas City, MO 64116.

For the purist collector, nothing can equal Scott Duff's two-volume set on the old rifle: *The M1 Garand of World War Two* and *The M1 Garand: Post World War Two.*

The following two are inexpensive items, primarily useful for the shooter:

Rifle, National Matches. United States Army Weapons & Munitions Command, 1963. (Usually about $4.95.)

The M1 Rifle. National Rifle Association Publications, Washington, D.C., revised in 1985. ($3.95)

The books listed below demonstrate and explain the Garand and the principles behind the rifle. There are other publications with better technical illustrations, but these two contain a lot of information for a reasonable price. They are somewhat dated, and there are some research errors (easily corrected by referral to GCA publications).

Book of the Garand, Maj. Gen. Julian S. Hatcher. Infantry Journal Press, Washington, D.C. Updated in 1977.

Know Your M1 Garand, E.J. Hoffschmidt. Blacksmith Publishers, Chino Valley, AZ, 1975.

Many retired armorers retain copies of various War Department/Department of Defense Technical Operations Orders and manuals that pertain to specific parts and procedures. These are worth copying.

APPENDIX II
THE MARKETPLACE

As in *The Complete M1 Garand*, "The Marketplace" comprises mainly names and addresses, along with notes, so that you can find most of what's been discussed in the text.

The only place to get much selection in custom M1 Garand stocks in laminate and various grades of walnut is

Boyd's Gunstock Industries, Inc.
25376 403rd Avenue
Mitchell, SD 57301

Century produces M1 receivers, and if the current edict changes, may even begin importing them again. They also import PMP and a wide variety of surplus ammo, most notably the British Radway Green I like so well.

Century Arms, Inc.
1161 Holland Drive
Boca Raton, FL 33487

There is no more Department of Civilian Marksmanship, but there is a private firm, sort of, with considerable volunteer help, that ships M1s and various other items, including parts, and now offers grades of M1s. Gone are the 18-month waits, but also gone are the very low prices of the early 1980s. Partly gone, too, is the direct NRA affiliation, though one of the ways to qualify is still via an accredited high-power competition program. For literature, contact

The Civilian Marksmanship Program
P.O. Box 576
Fort Clinton, OH 43452

Barrels such as those tested here on my 1.4 million rifle are available, along with lots of other M1 goodies and barrels in higher grade, from

Fulton Armory, Incorporated
Bollman Place #1
Savage, MD 20763

The Garand Collector's Association is almost essential for the serious Garand collector, and handy even for shooters.

The Garand Collector's Association
P.O. Box 7498
North Kansas City, MO 64116

Even if Krieger doesn't produce the best M1 Garand barrel in the world, I haven't seen the one that's better.

Krieger Barrels, Inc.
N114 W. 18697 Clinton Drive
Germantown, WI 53022

Derrick Martin is one of my primary consultants and my favorite smith. And unlike a lot of gunsmiths, he's also still an active competitor.

Derrick Martin
Accuracy Speaks Gunsmithing

A very heavy Krieger barrel, mounted on a Smith-refinished H&R receiver, in one of Boyd's laminated M1 Garand stocks.

3960 North Usery Pass Road
Mesa, AZ 85207

Midway has offered reloading supplies to dealers for a long time and has branched out. It owns the Bishop and Fajen names, though there is not much likelihood that there will be new product in the future. It also sells wood and accessories for the M1, including Boyd's, and features, in stock, such items as Kager's M1 hooded duplex reticle front sight.

MIDWAY
5875 W. Van Horn Tavern Road
Columbia, MO 65203

MPI produces the only commonly available M1 polymer stock I know of.

MPI
5655 NW Street
P.O. Box 83266
Portland, OR 97383-0266

Bob Reese is one of the pioneers of M1 research and collecting. And his firm, RSI, still handles a considerable variety of M1 goodies. Bob, an avid collector himself, is looking, in particular, for anything related to Italian M1 sniper rifles.

RSI, Inc.
25132 Ridge Road
Colona, IL 61241

There is probably nobody who handles more Garand parts than Sarco.

Sarco, Inc.
323 Union Street
Stirling, NJ 07980

Smith produces some M1 products, does high-quality dark-phosphate finishing, produces M14 receivers, and provides full-service M1 smithing. Smith also stocks many M1 parts.

Smith Arms International

Above: One of Smith's dark-phosphate refinishing operations delivered this H&R in a nearly black color, quite close to its very late original finish.

1701 W. 10th Street #14
Tempe, AZ 85281

Springfield Armory, Incorporated, is a former manufacturer of M1 Garand cast receivers and provider of some services regarding the rifle.

Springfield Armory, Inc.
420 W. Main Street
Geneseo, IL 61254

Larry Stewart operates a well-ordered store full of fascinating military antiques and curios, to include a vast selection of items pertinent to the M1 Garand and other U.S. and foreign firearms.

Stewart's Military Antiques
108 West Main Street
Mesa, AZ 85201

Mail to:
P.O. Box 1492
Mesa, AZ 85211-1492
The finest, custom-made, specially marked M1907 variant slings such as the items pictured herein can be had from

Leslie Tam
1411 St. Louis Drive
Honolulu, HI 96816

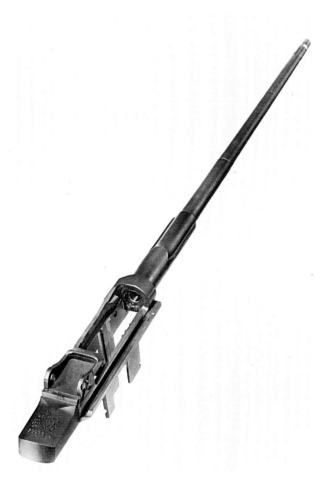

Right: Apparently, Springfield Armory, Incorporated will soon begin to deliver new cast receivers.

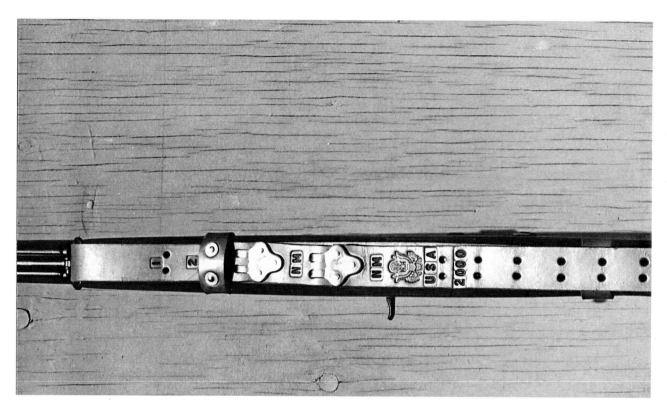

One of Leslie Tam's logoed custom M1907 slings.

The Garand is itself a tribute to the citizens who made it, the genius who designed it, and the creative, mostly civilian troopers who lugged it to victory in so many horrible places so very long ago. But this rifle is far from being a mere monument, and the accomplishments of that generation and the rifle must be recognized and reinvigorated.

Enjoy!